↝ The ↜
Chronic Fatigue
Syndrome
COOKBOOK

~ The ~ Chronic Fatigue Syndrome COOKBOOK

Delicious and Wellness-Enhancing Recipes Created Especially for CFS Sufferers

by
Mary Hale and Chris Miller

Introduction by Murray Susser, M.D.

A BIRCH LANE PRESS BOOK
Published by Carol Publishing Group

60, 665   8-94   18.95

A Birch Lane Press Book
Published by Carol Publishing Group
Birch Lane Press is a registered trademark of Carol Communications, Inc.
Editorial Offices: 600 Madison Avenue, New York, N.Y. 10022
Sales and Distribution Offices: 120 Enterprise Avenue, Secaucus, N.J. 07094
In Canada: Canadian Manda Group, P.O. Box 920, Station U, Toronto, Ontario
   M8Z 5P9
Queries regarding rights and permissions should be addressed to Carol Publishing Group, 600 Madison Avenue, New York, N.Y. 10022

Carol Publishing books are available at special discounts for bulk purchases, sales promotions, fund-raising, or educational purposes. Special editions can be created to specifications. For details, contact Special Sales Department, Carol Publishing Group, 120 Enterprise Avenue, Secaucus, N.J. 07094

Manufactured in the United States of America
10 9 8 7 6 5 4 3 2 1

Library of Congress Cataloging-in-Publication Data

Hale, Mary, 1953–
    The chronic fatigue syndrome cookbook : delicious and wellness-
enhancing recipes created especially for CFS sufferers / by Mary
Hale and Chris Miller; introduction by Murray Susser.
    p. cm.
    ISBN 1-55972-220-7
    1. Chronic fatigue syndrome—Diet therapy—Recipes. I. Miller,
Chris, 1942–   . II. Title.
RB150.F37H35   1994
641.5'63—dc20   93-43775
                                                        CIP

∽ Contents ∾

PART THREE

The Phase Two Diet

APPENDIX

Food You Don't Cook Yourself

Introduction

I am glad Mary and Chris have written this book. It fills an important niche in my treatment plan for Chronic Fatigue Syndrome (CFS) patients. If you have CFS but your doctor is not nutritionally oriented, this is the book for you.

The recipes herein flow simply and tastefully. I find that even a clumsy kitchen oaf such as I can negotiate them. And, once created, these nourishing and appetizing delicacies delight the palate and refresh the spirit, easing the burden which this disease inflicts on the simple need to eat.

If you have CFS, it is more important than ever to eat simply and safely. It may well be that a major reason people develop CFS is their failure to eat well. I believe this book can give the CFS victim some of the pleasure of eating which often disappears in the face of dealing with CFS. Mary and Chris, from their personal experience, have tempered the problems that CFS caused them, not merely coping with the need to eat, but once more having food be a treat as well as a treatment.

I have been treating CFS patients many years—actually for fifteen years before Chronic Fatigue Syndrome was even named. Since co-authoring the book *Solving the Puzzle of Chronic Fatigue Syndrome*, I have treated such patients in greater numbers. My belief that CFS is a disease of the immune system has been continually reaffirmed. My consequent belief—that the immune system can be fully treated only by giving strict attention to nutrition—has also been continually reaffirmed.

Deciding upon the best diet in this complex world of modern eating is a problem that would have taxed the proverbial wisdom of Solomon. Arguments and controversy abound. No one is quite sure what the ideal diet should be for a healthy, normal human, much less for one with CFS. Experience has taught us that the principles and techniques of this book work. We may not always know exactly *why* they work, but success should be the touchstone, and we have experienced success with this approach.

I know little about the nitty-gritty of preparing recipes, planning a meal, or shopping for ingredients. Instructing a patient on the fine points of these skills, therefore, has never been my strong suit. But I do know a considerable amount about reading labels, and which foods are good or bad for people with CFS and related problems. My role in making this book useful to CFS patients, then, is to explain how food and menu selection can support the immune and endocrine systems as they claw their way back to health. I have been prescribing diet selection for virtually every patient I have seen during the past twenty years—over 15,000 of them. That certainly gives me the right to claim a modicum of experience.

When planning the nutritional management of CFS patients, I consider many factors: sugar metabolism, weight status, digestive and bowel function, allergic status, and the function of digestive endocrines such as the pancreas and liver. I must also consider what is possible; the patient's taste, energy, resources, and willingness to accept new eating habits all add to the equation which must be solved. Planning a diet with all these considerations can drive one to distraction and probably will never result in perfection. We must always settle for some compromise.

At this point, it is well to describe CFS. Chronic Fatigue Syndrome is a disease of some mystery. It has probably been around forever, but has only become recognized and named since the mid-1980s. There is not yet a test that proves a person has CFS (it is not Epstein-Barr virus). CFS, therefore, remains a disease we clinically identify by exclusion. That is, we diagnose by the patient's history and physical exam, and exclude other possible diseases, which can be identified by testing. Lyme Disease, hepatitis, mononucleosis, thyroiditis, and literally thousands more could present themselves with most of the provisional characteristics assigned to CFS by the Center for Disease Control. This government agency in Atlanta has described eleven such characteristics. If a patient suffers at least eight of them, and has no other disease which could explain the symptoms, that person has CFS.

Major criteria (both must be present):

1. The new onset of a debilitating fatigue which persists in a steady or relapsing course for at least six months and curtails average daily activity by more than 50 percent.

2. The exclusion of other medical conditions that produce similar complaints, including auto-immune diseases such as rheumatoid arthritis, chronic infections—viral or nonviral (caused by bacteria, yeast, or parasites), AIDS or related diseases, psychiatric disorders, neuromuscular disorders, hormonal disorders, etc.

Minor criteria (eight of eleven must be present):
1. Low-grade fever or chills
2. Sore throat
3. Swollen glands
4. Muscle aches
5. Muscle weakness
6. Joint aches
7. Sleep disturbance
8. Exercise intolerance
9. Neurologic problems (mental confusion, memory loss, or emotional imbalance)
10. Headache
11. Sudden onset of symptom complex

Malaise (sick feeling) is not included in the criteria but should be. Feeling sick is an almost universal symptom in CFS. Commonly, CFS patients suffer from bowel and other digestive upsets (often related to candida yeast infections). Allergic symptoms to food and inhalants such as mold are also common.

Let us take a closer look at candida, which has a number of implications for CFS patients. Candida is a yeast that is best known for causing vaginal infections. Most commonly, candida vaginitis occurs following a course of antibiotics. It may be uncomfortable and annoying but does not usually cause major upset unless it becomes persistent and recurrent. This most common yeast problem overshadows other obvious but less common candida problems, such as thrush (yeast infection of the tongue) and diarrhea, which can also follow a course of antibiotics. Both the vaginitis and the diarrhea (and probably thrush as well) result from biological imbalance caused by the antibiotics killing off the normal, friendly bacteria which live in the vagina and the bowel. Medical doctors readily recognize these conditions and have effective remedies for them. However, they often do not see the more controversial connection between yeast infections and CFS.

Candida yeast has, for over a decade, been increasingly recognized as causing a syndrome very similar to CFS. Many supposed CFS patients actually recover when treated for candida. These patients do not have CFS in the true definition, but the connection between CFS and candida is tightly interwoven in many of them. The connection can be extremely complex to explain. To simplify without going into unnecessary detail, let me say that there are three important elements to the connection between CFS and candida:

1. Candida can cause a syndrome that is virtually identical to CFS. The major difference is that candida can be diagnosed and treated specifically with relative ease.

2. Candida infection in the gut or vagina can be present along with CFS, but not be the entire problem. Treating the candida, therefore, may result in improvement but not entire resolution of the problem.

3. Candida infection can create an allergy to the candida organism and subsequently cause cross allergy to other yeast such as baker's yeast. This is perhaps the most confounding aspect of the problem because of the sneakiness of it. A person with CFS may get a reaction from eating bread because of a chain of events which began with taking antibiotics, which led to a yeast infection, which led to a candida allergy, which led to a baker's yeast allergy.

The yeast allergy leads to some of the most annoying restrictions in the diet. When the allergy causes clear symptoms, the patient must avoid the allergic food and take other steps such as desensitization, rotation diet, etc. One of the unfortunate results of this problem has been the unnecessarily restrictive yeast diet. Many writers and doctors do not make it clear that you *cannot get a yeast infection from eating yeast.* Baker's yeast, mushrooms, vinegar, and so forth *do not cause infections.* The only yeast infection in this scenario is from candida. Other yeast and fungi should be dietetically avoided *only if you are allergic to them.* To be sure, it may be difficult to determine allergy because of the complexities of immediate and delayed hypersensitivity reactions as well as the fluctuations which may occur and the intricate interactions between allergic foods.

I know that this does not truly simplify the diet picture of candida and CFS patients. If you just understand that there is infection from candida and allergy potential from all the other yeast which is in our diet, you should be able to act appropriately and seek proper assistance.

As you can see, CFS and its associated problems can tax the patient and the physician to the limit. The patient suffers a debilitating condition which eludes diagnostic certainty, thereby leaving him or her with a frustrating illness that cannot be proven, and for which there is no satisfactory medical treatment. Most physicians now use antidepressant drugs such as doxepin and anti-ulcer drugs such as ranitidine. These and an enormous list of other medicants have given occasional relief, but little hope of a cure.

I follow a medical philosophy, now represented by hundreds of doctors and other health care providers, which espouses a treatment plan for the immune system. By that I mean using nutrition and other natural methods of healing which work in concert with medical treatments such as antibiotic drugs, gamma globulin, Kutapressin and other fairly standard medical (though sometimes obscure) modalities.

For further information about this complex subject, I modestly recommend the aforementioned book I wrote with Dr. Michael Rosenbaum: *Solving the Puzzle of Chronic Fatigue Syndrome*, published by Life Sciences Press in Tacoma, Washington. Obviously, I can only dent the surface of this subject here.

This introduction mainly explains the reasons for the diet principles used in designing recipes. When I talk about diet to my patients, the question I most often hear is "Why?" Why no sugar? Why no fruit? Why no milk? Many of the diet principles foment argument. Many people talk of the yeast-free diet and the low-fat diet and an endless parade of pros and cons about the various aspects of nutritional eating. But it need not be complex; a few simple principles can make your diet measurably healthier and you won't have to be a Nobel Laureate to understand it.

Sugar, for example, is a major culprit. The average American eats about 125 pounds of the stuff in his or her yearly diet. That is 125 pounds too much. Sugar masquerades as food, but could rightly be called a drug with calories. It contains no nutrients— just calories. And since calories abound in the American diet while every other nutrient goes begging, sugar may actually poison us insidiously.

That may sound like a harsh indictment of the treat we use to reward children. We know, however, that we need nutrients like vitamins B1 and B6 and pantothenic acid to burn sugar. Those nutrients get processed out of the sugar cane or sugar beet from which sugar comes. When the processed sugar reaches us in candy or pastry or ice cream (and more insidiously, in our canned, packaged, and frozen foods), our bodies need to use the reserve nutrients to metabolize the sugar. If the reserve nutrients are marginal or lacking (which is likely after prolonged sugar usage), we soon create a deficiency state—usually a subtle one at first. The first signs of such deficiency may be colds, flus, rashes, allergies, muscle aches, etc. Next would come, perhaps, emotional states like depression. Next we will likely see hypoglycemia (low blood sugar) and a more serious immune deficiency such as pneumonia. It begins to look as if CFS acts like a flu that never got better. What if it were that simple? What if CFS is nothing more than an ordinary cold or flu virus that got into the body and the immune system was not up to kicking the bug out, which ordinarily would take only a week or two? Does this scenario make the relationship between diet and CFS more logical? I think it does.

Let us now address additional foods which we feel are important to eliminate in order to bring us better health and less CFS. For example, why no processed grains? It happens that white flour and white rice, to name two of the most abundant ones, are little more than chains of nutritionless sugars. Starches in general are chains of sugars, but the starch in the farina of a whole grain of wheat is the king in a court of juicy nutrients, most of which are destroyed in the refining process. The whole wheat berry contains the germ and the bran along with the farina. When the refining of wheat removes the germ, which contains most of the vitamins, and the bran, which contains the protein and minerals, we are left with the farina—which is then bleached to kill any semblance of life that may have survived the milling. Add to the farina eight synthetic B vitamins which are made from coal tar, and we get "enriched" flour. Was ever a word used more deceptively than "enriched"?

Although we owe a great debt to the refining process, there are some problems. When we learned to polish rice, we created epidemics of beri-beri in the Orient. Prior to that, the Orientals lived on natural whole rice, which gave them reasonably good health. After "polished" rice, which is perhaps slightly less evil than "enriched" flour, impoverished peasants who lived on this cheap convenience developed more of the major diseases of civilization. Beri-beri and heart disease became epidemic. In those days, no one had yet named CFS, but I bet it was common.

The principle now begins to take shape. Refined food, which pleases our acquired tastes, gradually robs us of our nutritional reserve. Generally the more primitive the food source, the more nourishment it will provide. This book, as well as my basic therapeutic diet, recommends the use of whole wheat, un-polished rice, and all other grains in the most primitive state available. I have seen this principle alone make major differences in a person's health.

Milk restrictions surprise many people. Until recently, milk enjoyed the best public relations of almost any food. In recent years, it has suffered the slings of the anticholesterol campaign. But milk carries a lot more anti-nutritional baggage than most people suspect. Fat and cholesterol are not significant evils in CFS. The larger problem is milk sugar. Milk is very sweet. The lactose sugar in milk actually rivals the sucrose (table sugar) which permeates our pastries, ice cream, and candy. It behaves much like a processed sugar—especially in low-fat milk! The fat in whole milk acts to buffer the sugar so that it does not absorb so quickly into the bloodstream. If you must drink milk, select whole milk (unless you have a serious cholesterol problem).

Another problem with milk is that the protein in it seems to trigger allergic reactions in many susceptible people. The al-lergies may be garden-variety respiratory or skin, or, more insidiously, may affect the brain, the gut, and evidently the immune system. These allergies often go unrecognized, and many orthodox medicine physicians disagree as to whether they even exist. There are even more problems with milk and milk products, but I shall not belabor the point. The best policy with milk products seems to be total avoidance at first and moderate, intermittent use once the problem comes under control. In my medical office, we often do skin testing for milk and other foods to find the precise allergy and the appropriate treatment for that allergy.

That fruit may be harmful is another surprise to most people. Why avoid fruit? It comes to us fresh and raw. One of our most primitive and, therefore, desirable foods should not threaten our health. Alas, it contains a lot of sugar, and that sugar can be a problem for a damaged metabolism. It changes the acidity in the gut and absorbs quickly into the bloodstream. It peaks the blood sugar abruptly and requires many nutrients to metabolize it. It probably causes yeast to grow and metabolize more quickly, thereby increasing any toxicity that may be occurring from excess yeast growth in the gut. I tell people that fruit should be treated like exercise. Exercise is good for you unless you have a broken leg or some such injury. Fruit is good for you unless you have a broken metabolism. After you heal, you can have all you want.

Incidentally, for some people, potato behaves like fruit. The starch in the potato breaks down into sugar in the mouth and hits the stomach like pure table sugar. It does not taste sweet, but it behaves like a sweet. Be alert. Some people can handle potato; others can't. Sweet potato, to make things even more confusing, is okay. It has oils in it and doesn't seem to attack our sugar balance. Yet people frequently eat potato, but avoid sweet potato, because the sweet potato seems sweeter.

Food allergy plays a major role for many CFS patients. Why should anyone be allergic to food? Food allergy seems to result from a combination of two digestive errors. First, the food does not break down completely into its basic component parts. Protein, for example, should digest into individual amino acids which are easily absorbed into the bloodstream and are virtually never allergenic. If they are not completely digested, they result in chains of amino acids called polypeptides. These polypeptides are highly allergenic, but would not cause any problem if the second digestive error did not occur. The second error has to do with the absorptive function of the bowel wall. If the bowel becomes damaged and dysfunctional for any reason, it may absorb these highly allergenic polypeptides. This combination of errors commonly occurs.

I see many CFS patients with such afflictions from simple food. They may be difficult to recognize because the allergic response can take several forms. It can be "immediate," which means it occurs in minutes, or more insidiously, it can be "delayed." Delayed hypersensitivities may not manifest for several days. This makes them almost impossible to detect by simple self-observation. Food allergy requires much more discussion than we can allow here, but anyone with a reasonable suspicion of suffering such a condition should definitely have it checked by an expert physician.

Alcohol and caffeine are two legal drugs which give a great deal of pleasure and have their uses. They can also do a great deal of damage when used to excess. Deciding how much is too much is a difficult question for a healthy person. With a CFS sufferer, the answer is usually painfully obvious: Most CFS patients cannot tolerate *any* caffeine or alcohol. Caffeine may give a temporary boost, but often delivers a devastating backlash. Similarly, alcohol can provide some temporary tranquility, but afterwards usually hits us with horrible weakness and fatigue. Most CFS patients quickly recognize the sting of alcohol and give it up themselves. For many, it is more difficult relinquishing caffeine. But it is important to find a way to wean from it. When I say wean, I mean it. I usually recommend decreasing by not more than 25 percent of the daily intake each week and taking three to six weeks to get off it entirely. Quitting cold turkey usually results in temporary headaches and increased fatigue. You can soften the blow by taking good vitamin supplements (after consulting with your doctor). That is sometimes the most important part of managing the weaning process.

On the subject of nutritional supplements, I want to say that I believe they are a vital part of treating CFS. Many practitioners who treat CFS now clearly recognize the need for more vitamins and minerals than we can get from the best possible diet. I have been prescribing vitamin and mineral supplements for twenty-five years. I do so because my experience has been undeniably positive. The medical journals have more and more validated my experience. For decades, I have heard that my routine use of thirty or more vitamin pills per day has been controversial at best, and many went so far as to call it quackery. Now studies from UCLA, Harvard, and other prestigious institutions are showing that supplements can cure as well as prevent disease. The purpose of this book is not to teach you about supplemental vitamins, but I would be remiss if I did not inform you of their importance. An excellent diet must be present for CFS patients to recover, but do not forget that most will also need supplements.

I conclude my introduction with a wish for your wellness. I believe that the principles and techniques of this cookbook will make an enormous contribution to any CFS sufferer who uses it appropriately. Just remember that the raw materials of our immune system come only from food. If you use poor building materials, you will get a poor building.

MURRAY SUSSER, M.D.
Santa Monica, California

A Note From Mary Hale, CFS Sufferer

In 1984, I contracted Chronic Fatigue Syndrome. To manage the disease and live my life while slowly regaining my health has been the biggest challenge I have ever faced. If you have CFS or some other immune system dysfunction, you know what I mean—simply getting out of bed in the morning can be like climbing Mount Everest. Taking care of children, having a career, making dinner—in short, having a normal life—are often close to impossible. But I found that eventually I could do it, and though at times I despaired of ever achieving my goal, I have, in fact, regained my health. It wasn't an easy journey, but it's over, and I'm happy to say I have a better, richer life than when I started. You can, too.

But this book was not written only for CFS sufferers. It's really for *everybody* whose health problems require them to eat better. This book is even for those who wish to lose weight, avoid sugar and dairy products, or eliminate MSG and preservatives from their diet. In short, this book can help you eat healthier and minimize the damage done by the ravages of time and the everyday difficulties of living.

I want to share with you one of the great secrets of life: Eating well can make you happy. Without caffeine to rev up, alcohol to wind down, and all the other impurities we commonly put in our systems, you can discover who you really are. You can maintain your ideal weight and ward off a variety of diseases.

I welcome you to the new life that can come with this book. Read it, enjoy the recipes. Take what works for you and discard the rest. You'll usher in a new regime of health. Enjoy!

A Note From Chris Miller,
Spouse of a CFS Sufferer

For me, eating is about pleasure. The three most important events of my day are breakfast, lunch, and dinner. I *love* food.

Over the years, I realized that if I *really* wanted to eat well, I'd have to learn how to cook for myself—what I could get at restaurants too often disappointed me. So I became a pretty fair chef. I learned how to whip up French sauces, Italian pastas, sweet Thai concoctions, Japanese sushi, and American cheeseburgers, cookies, and cakes.

Imagine my horror when I found out my wife—the woman I plan to spend the rest of my life with—had contracted some weird disease that would allow her to eat none of the above! In fact, her list of forbidden foods looked nine miles long, while what she *could* eat seemed restricted to rice cakes, nut butter, and air.

I felt bad for her, but also for myself. How was I going to survive on this diet she had to follow so scrupulously? Was my greatest pleasure to be taken from me?

But no. What I discovered was that a perfectly delicious menu of foods was still very much achievable, despite the necessity of staying within the parameters of the Diet. It took time, and was sometimes frustrating, but I was able to assemble a large number of tasty, healthy recipes—which I now pass on to you.

Ironically, I wound up *preferring* this diet to my old one, with its rich sauces and so forth. I feel better, look better, lost weight, and have fewer worries about cholesterol and today's other nutritional bugaboos. So, in my dogged pursuit of hedonistic dining—in spite of Mary's health problems—I actually wound up improving my own physical and emotional well-being!

And as for *you*, this book will make it possible to eat well, despite your unfortunate problem. *Bon appétit!*

～ The ～
Chronic Fatigue
Syndrome
COOKBOOK

PART ONE

Getting Oriented

❦ 1 ❧

Diet and Chronic Fatigue Syndrome

So you have Chronic Fatigue Syndrome. The disease is not yet completely understood. But those who have it are all too familiar with the pain and unending difficulty it puts into their daily lives.

What *is* known about CFS is that it probably consists of a mixture of components, including one or more viruses, out-of-control yeast growth (candida), allergies, and a weakened immune system.

Although doctors, OMDs (Doctors of Oriental Medicine), acupuncturists, and other health care providers differ on how to treat the disease, one thing about which they almost all agree is that a special diet is essential to getting better.

The CFS diet should:

(1) Avoid all substances that are generally held to be unhealthy: sugar, alcohol, fried foods, etc.

(2) Eliminate all substances to which you are allergic.

Most people with CFS also suffer from allergies—there's a high correspondence between the two. Your physician can help determine what your allergies are. *You will particularly need to determine whether you have contracted a systemic yeast infection known as candida. If you have, you will be susceptible to a number of cross-allergies that could rule out baker's yeast, mushrooms, vinegar, and other foods.*

3

The recipes in this cookbook adhere to these rules. We realize that health care professionals will differ on what foods should and should not be allowed in your diet. That's why the ingredients we use here are conservative, and should do you no harm, no matter what combination of factors is causing your particular version of CFS.

The Bad News and the Good News

No way around it, you're faced with a double whammy. Not only is a chronic disease making you miserable, there's this stringent new diet you have to follow as well. The list of things you're not allowed to eat is long, and certain to contain at least three dozen items you can't live without. And when you see the list of what you *can* eat, you'll wonder "How can I possibly survive on this!?"

When you're so tired that brushing your teeth can seem like running a marathon, the job of revamping the entire way you eat seems impossible. Foods you've taken for granted all your life are suddenly verboten: The frozen dinners you popped in the microwave on nights you got home late contain sugar and other taboo ingredients; the wine you liked with lamb chops is mainly distilled sugar; you can't eat pizza (cheese), or take-out Chinese (MSG, soy sauce), or one single thing at McDonald's (sugar, cheese, God knows what else).

The world, you quickly discover, is not set up for people with Chronic Fatigue Syndrome.

But here's the good news: With a little thought and planning, and the help of this book, creating new eating habits isn't nearly the insurmountable task you think it is. *Not only can you eat healthily, you can eat well.*

The recipes contained herein are as normal as scrambled eggs, green salads, and pasta. It's bad enough you don't feel well—you don't need to endure a "health food" (to many people, a code for "bland" or "weird") diet as well. Your authors are mainstream food lovers, not self-denying health obsessives trying to force you to live on bean sprouts and tofu. The recipes in this book would appeal to any lover of food and eating.

Your Diet's Two Phases

Most doctors and health care professionals who treat CFS ask their patients to radically change their diet. As we have already discussed, good nutrition is vital to regaining health—and maintaining it.

That's why there are two phases to the CFS diet. Phase One is for those who have just been diagnosed or are one of the 10 percent who are hardest hit (ask your doctor if this applies to you).

The most important thing to do in the Phase One portion of the diet is to eliminate all preservatives, sugar, caffeine, and allergy-causing foods from your body. As you do this, your immune system will become stronger and you will become better. Eating "bad" food can only make you sicker— and you certainly don't need that!

For this reason, the Phase One diet is the more restrictive one. Most of the recipes in this book are for Phase One. (Don't worry, they still taste great.) You'll be adhering to this diet for at least four months, possibly longer. Once you've reachieved a certain degree of wellness, experiencing more good days than bad and an increased energy throughout most of the day, you can move on to Phase Two.

A few words of warning here: In the beginning, the cleansing process makes some people feel worse. But as the diet "kicks in," you will experience a return of mental clarity and physical energy you'd almost forgotten you could feel. It's then you'll discover what this diet can truly mean for you.

By the time you get to the Phase Two portion of the diet, you should be stronger and healthier. Your body should be ready to tolerate "good" foods such as the natural sugar in certain fruits.

Only you and your doctor or nutritionist will know which newly introduced foods will work for you. It's a matter of trial and error or even testing. For instance, it's possible that you will always be allergic to bananas and should never eat them. But other fruits, goat's milk yogurt, and wheat products may be just fine. It's really an individual matter. At this point, you will certainly be ready for more diversity in your diet and you deserve it.

Again, the recipes in the Phase One diet are for the first four months of your diet. Of course, you can continue to use them throughout your treatment or, for that matter, your life. Also, many of the recipes can easily be converted to the Phase Two diet; in the case of pasta, for instance, merely substitute wheat pasta for wheatless. The point is, if from now on you ate only the strictest recipes, you wouldn't feel deprived in the slightest. They're delicious, they're easy, and they'll make you feel great!

Here's the list of what you can and can't eat. Make a copy and take it shopping with you. Don't worry, you'll soon have it memorized. And remember—*always read ingredient lists.*

Forbidden Foods

1. *Sugar* A.k.a sucrose, glucose, fruit sugar, dextrose, dextrins, dextran, diastase, diastatic malt, ethyl maltol, sorbitol, corn sweeteners, caramel, carob syrup, fructose, high-fructose corn syrup, honey, molasses, brown sugar, fruit juice, maple syrup, brown rice syrup, steria, etc. This also includes artificial sweeteners—Nutrasweet, Sweet 'n Low, and the like. Sugar is the *number one* item you must avoid. *If you do nothing else, eliminate this from your diet.*

2. *Milk Products* Milk, cream, cheese, yogurt, sour cream, ice cream, etc. (The exception is butter, which is no problem.) The reason for this is simple: Milk products contain sugar, plus many people are allergic to them. For the Phase One diet, this includes goat's milk products as well.

3. *Yeast-Containing Foods* If you're allergic to them. That means tofu and miso. Also anything fermented—beer, wine, sake, champagne, soy sauce, vinegar. Also most breads, rolls, cakes, and so forth; yeast is what makes them rise.

4. *Alcohol* It's best to stay away from alcohol completely, but when you don't, use tequila or vodka, and do so in moderation.

5. *Mushrooms* If you have an allergy to mushrooms or yeast, watch out. Fungi are made of mold, which is what yeast is. If you're not allergic, you can eat mushrooms whenever you like—especially try the shiitake mushroom. This wonderful-tasting delicacy may even have immune-stimulating characteristics.

6. *All Fruits* They're too sweet, and many contain yeast and ferment easily. Fruit juice, even freshly squeezed, is also forbidden. However, when you reach Phase Two of your diet, try reintroducing fruits one at a time and see if you can tolerate them.

7. *Tea and Coffee* This includes decaffeinated teas and coffee. Herbal teas are okay, however. Especially pau d'arco, which you can find at health food stores. This tea from South America may actually kill yeast.

8. *Commercial Mustards and Mayonnaise* Store-bought mustards and mayonnaise contain vinegar, a definite no-no for the many CFS patients who are allergic to the yeast in it. Try making your own mayonnaise using lemon juice instead of vinegar.

9. *Fried Foods*

10. *Wheat and Rye*   Again only if you're allergic. Of course, most crackers, cereals, pastas, breads, etc. are made from wheat flour. However, if you don't have an allergy to wheat, don't deny yourself.

11. *Catsups, Tomato Sauces, Barbecue Sauces*   Unless you make your own without vinegar, syrup, or sugar.

12. *Miscellaneous No-Nos*   Horseradish, oatmeal, potatoes.

Allowed Foods

1. *Poultry*   Chicken, duck, goose, pheasant, turkey, chicken liver, and liver pâté.

2. *Most Fish*   Abalone, bass, bluefish, carp, catfish, caviar, clam, crab, cod, eel, flounder, haddock, halibut, herring, lobster, mackerel*, oyster, perch, pike, pollock, salmon (fresh*), oyster, sardines, scallops, shad*, shrimp, smelt, snails, snapper, swordfish**, trout*, tuna**, wakeme, whitefish*.

3. *All Vegetables and Fresh Vegetable Juices*

4. *Selected Fruits and Fresh-Squeezed Fruit Juices* It's best to avoid all fruits until you're on the Phase Two diet. When you're ready try papaya, mango, kiwi, pineapple, banana, honeydew melon, coconut, guava, lemons, limes. Also the juices of these, and unsweetened cranberry juice. Best to eat these fruits only in the morning.

6. *Grains and Beans*   Whole, unprocessed brown rice, wild rice, millet, buckwheat, quinoa, and amaranth.

---

*High fat
**High mercury

Avoid white rice. It's best to combine grains and beans to make a complete protein.

7. *Butter and eggs*

8. *Nuts*   Except peanuts and pistachios, which harbor mold.

9. *Rice Cakes, Rice Crackers (made from whole unprocessed rice), Corn Tortillas, Corn Chips, Popcorn*

10. *Rice Noodles, Japanese Buckwheat Noodles, Quinoa Pasta, Corn Pasta, Amaranth Pasta*

11. *Meat*   Lamb, veal, rabbit. Limit to just two servings per week due to fat and difficulty of digestion. Avoid processed meats such as sausage, ham, and bacon.

A Note About Salt

We haven't included salt in any of our recipes. Trying to cleave to the healthiest possible approach, we have left the decision to use salt or not up to you. Dr. Susser believes that only if you have heart trouble, hypertension, or a bad problem with water retention do you need to worry about salt. In fact, he says, many who pursue health and fitness make the mistake of cutting *too* much salt out of their diet. Salt in moderation is good.

Many of the recipes herein are greatly improved in the flavor department by the addition of salt. So feel free to add some as you cook, or sprinkle some at the table. Our number one priority, after feeding you nothing that can hurt you, is feeding you meals that are delicious and can reintroduce sensual pleasure to your life, even if you are sick.

SUBSTITUTIONS

When a recipe contains ingredients that seem to remove it from consideration, maybe you can use substitutes. Here's a by-no-means exhaustive list of substitutions that have worked for us.

Recipe Calls For:	*Instead Use:*
Milk	Goat's milk*; coconut milk
Cheese	Goat cheese*
Yogurt	Goat's milk yogurt*
Vinegar	Lemon juice
Mayonnaise	Homemade (see Chapter 8)
Flour (wheat)	Amaranth, barley, brown rice, buckwheat, millet, oat, quinoa, rice, and soy flours
White wine	Chicken broth
Bread	Tortillas or other unleavened bread (corn tortillas, if you can't have wheat), ponce bread, and rice bread
Pasta	Rice noodles, Japanese buckwheat noodles, quinoa pasta, corn pasta, amaranth pasta

---

*For Phase Two diet only

A Coping Strategy

What you are about to undertake—the overhaul of your eating habits—is not easy. The following may help.

There will be times when you'll be too tired even to *think* about cooking. That's when you go to the freezer for a meal you've cooked previously. Or throw together the ultra-easy, ultra-quick foods described in Chapter 4, "Mary's Quickies."

The number one rule is *avoid bad ingredients*. But this is a rule that can and probably should be broken once in a while. For the number two (and equally important) rule is, *be good to yourself*. We recommend adhering to Dr. Susser's 19-to-2 ratio—if nineteen of your twenty-one weekly meals are dietetically correct, give yourself a break on the other two. Yield to temptation and go for that slice of pepperoni pizza you've been mentally salivating over—the nurturing it'll do for your soul will probably outweigh whatever damage it does to your body. (Although, to be prudent about this, check out the impact of such forbidden foods—if they seem to hurt you, drop them.)

Though alcoholic beverages are inescapably on your forbidden list, even here you can give yourself the occasional treat. Vodka's safest. Stolichnaya, Absolut, or Icy are tasty and eye-opening. Try them on the rocks with a squeeze of lemon or lime or straight from the freezer—which renders them thick and oily—with buffalo grass or a grind of pepper.

Having CFS doesn't mean you've retired from the human race. The occasional forbidden pleasure reaffirms your humanity. Just don't make a habit of it.

Meanwhile, give yourself as many *allowed* pleasures as possible: hot tubs, massages, beautiful sunsets, and cut flowers. Managing CFS makes you enough of a self-denier by itself—compensate by developing an indulgent, generous relationship with yourself in other areas.

Stress, as has been widely noted, is one of the biggest blocks to maintaining good health. You must counterbalance its destructiveness. Unfortunately, this is difficult. Fatigue and depression can easily lead to bad eating habits, nonexercising, and total couch-potatohood. It becomes a horrible cycle. So be good to yourself. Ask your family and friends to help by taking you to the movies or for a gentle walk, or just sitting peacefully and reading a book to you. Loving care and compassion are some of the best medicines on your road to recovery.

~ 2 ~

Equipment

Because you're often tired, whatever makes life easier is good. Nonstick pots and pans, for instance. Electric can openers are also good. Wherever possible, simplify.

Freezer

You'll learn to exploit your freezer like never before. On nights you don't feel like cooking, pull something out that you cooked previously and froze in one- or two-person quantities. Get lots of those little plastic freezer containers and bags from the supermarket, and carry an inventory of selections at all times.

Microwave Ovens

A microwave is a big help. It can reheat your pau d'arco tea, cook vegetables and fish to perfection, warm your plates, boil water, melt butter, and resuscitate your dinner after interruptions by children or phones. We use one constantly.

We probably should not neglect to mention, however, that microwaves emit low-level electromagnetic fields. Studies have linked such fields to birth defects, miscarriage, and various forms of cancer. Though we don't let this cheery news bother us—and use the 'wave constantly anyway—we wanted you to have all the information you need to make your own decision.

Steamers

Steamers are the other great way to cook vegetables. Get one of the metal, fold-open ones. They're cheap, and you'll use it a lot.

Grill

An indoor grill on your cooktop is a great way to cook entire dinners that are healthy and easy. Outdoor grills are also fine—even a small hibachi will do the trick.

Juicer

One of your tickets back to health is freshly juiced vegetables, which turn out as a bonus to be delicious. If you don't have a juice bar situated around the corner, you might want to invest in one of these. Fresh vegetable juices are also available in health food stores (see Chapter 3).

Wok

Inexpensive and endlessly useful. Stir-frying is fast, easy, healthy, delicious, and fun. Those leftovers you have in the refrigerator can be thrown into the wok with a little oil and rice and voilà—instant lunch or dinner. You can wrap your creation in a warmed tortilla. Also good for making soups, eggs, sauces—almost anything.

Miscellaneous

Of course you'll need all the things any other cook needs—wooden spoons, a meat thermometer, a timer that goes *ping* when your food's ready. Food processors are very helpful—the time and aggravation they save make them worth the price. A Mouli grater works best for our grating needs.

Again, anything that makes life easier is good. A trash container with a foot pedal is better than one you have to open by hand. A sprayer attachment on your sink makes cleaning dishes a snap. Chopping boards keep the counters clean. Hand vacuums are great for dealing with dry spills. You get the idea.

In this spirit, please feel free to take as many shortcuts with these recipes as you like. Instead of peeling and seeding tomatoes, buy already peeled and seeded tomatoes in a can. If you don't have a particular ingredient on hand, be adventurous and substitute. Ask your butcher to cut and slice fish, poultry, and meat, so you don't have to. Take the shortcuts and just enjoy the nutritious, balanced diet this book can give you.

∾ 3 ∾

Shopping

Shopping's a whole new ballgame when there's an immune deficiency disease in your family. As with cooking and eating, you have to revamp your methodology. This may seem daunting at first. The extra label-reading is an annoyance. But, as with the other changes CFS forces on your life, you quickly incorporate it, and it becomes second nature.

Ingredient Lists

From now on, buy nothing until you've read the label. You won't *believe* the places sugar turns up. It's in bread and bacon, frozen french fries and tomato soup. It's in toothpaste and most chicken broths. It's even in many pain relievers.

There's milk in soda crackers and canned soups, yeast in sauerkraut and canned tomato sauce, wheat in liverwurst and bouillion cubes. It's a minefield out there.

What are you supposed to do? Read the ingredient lists. When you're buying ready-to-eat foods behind a deli counter, *ask* what the ingredients are. Be suspicious—more often than not it'll be justified.

By and large, you'll do better at health food stores than large commercial supermarkets. You're more likely to find what you're looking for—no sugar, no refined flour, no caffeine, and so forth. But even here you have to look out for the miso and honey. You must be endlessly vigilant.

You may wonder if there's anything that's *not* contaminated. As far as packaged, canned, and frozen foods are

16

concerned—very little. Whenever possible, use fresh ingredients and make your own food. When not possible, read labels carefully.

What ingredients should you be seeking to avoid? Here's a list. It's by no means exhaustive, but it covers the main areas. Copy and take it along while shopping until you've learned it.

Common Forbidden Ingredients

Aspartame
Beet juice concentrate
Corn syrup
Dextrose
Fructose
High fructose corn syrup
Hydrolyzed protein

Modified food
   starch
Potassium sorbate
Pyrophosphate
Sucrose
Sugar syrup
Yeast extract*

Common Foods to Avoid

Barbecue sauce
Beer
Bread*
Cakes
Cheese
Cookies
Cream
Crackers
Enriched flours
Mayonnaise
Milk

Olives
Pastries
Pickles
Pretzels
Rolls
Salad dressings
Sauerkraut
Soy sauce
Vinegar*
Wine

---

*You need to avoid these items only if you're allergic to them. However, since CFS patients so often are, the rule of thumb is: When in doubt, avoid them. We have, therefore, included no recipes containing these possible allergens in the Phase One section of this book.

Chicken Broth

One ingredient we'll call for again and again is chicken broth. There's a fairly easy recipe for chicken stock in Chapter 8. But if you're like us, you won't find time to make it very often. That's when you want to go to the canned chicken broth.

And when you do, you'll experience the ingredient problem in microcosm. Though there are many commercial chicken broths, most of them contain sugar! Two (that we've found) do not—Pritikin and Jewish Mother brand. Maybe you can discover others.

Going To Market

Shopping at the supermarket is an ordeal. Take it from one who has stood reading labels on endless packages while suffering every pain known to Chronic Fatigue sufferers—it's extremely difficult. But when you don't have the energy to cook, you're going to want something you can just heat up. Following are some ready-to-eat foods that for the most part fit the diet or maybe have only one questionable ingredient.

Again, this is not an exhaustive list, but it should help you identify the items that are the least harmful and in some rare cases actually good for you. The list is in two parts: foods generally found in your standard supermarket and those found in health food stores. It should come as no surprise where you'll have better luck.

Most of the brands listed below in the standard supermarket section are national brands, meaning you shouldn't have any trouble locating them no matter where you live in the United States.

SUPERMARKETS

Milk:

Meyenberg Goat's Milk

Snack Foods:

Amsnack Gourmet Rice Snax
Bell Natural Style Corn Chips (salt)
Chico San Sesame Rice Cakes or Popcorn Cakes
Hain Mini Popcorn Rice Cakes (salt)
Hain Butter-Flavored Popcorn (salt)
Eagle Lightly Salted Tortilla Chips (salt)
Jiffy Pop Natural Flavor Popcorn (salt)
Weight Watchers Popcorn (salt)

Salsas and Sauces:

El Pato Salsa De Jalapeno (salt)
Herdez Salsa Casera, mild, medium, and hot (salt)
Herdez Salsa Verde (salt)
Ortega Green Chile Salsa (salt)
Ortega Dried Jalapeños (salt)
Rosarita Enchilada Sauce (salt)

Cereals:

El Molino Puffed Corn
Kolln Oat Bran Crunch (barley malt)
Malt-O-Meal Puffed Rice
Mother's Oat Bran
Nabisco Cream of Rice
Quaker Oat Bran—look for the "no salt, no sugar" on
    the package

Soups:

Andersen's Split Pea Soup (salt)

Hain Vegetable Chicken Soup

Health Valley Fat-Free Soups:

Vegetable Barley

Real Italian Minestrone (whole wheat macaroni)

14 Garden Vegetable

Country Corn and Vegetable

Chicken Broth (grape juice)

Manhattan Clam Chowder (soy oil)

5 Bean Vegetable

Jewish Mother Chicken Broth

Jewish Mother Chicken Vegetable Soup (salt)

Jewish Mother Chicken Vegetable Rice (salt)

Pritikin Chicken Broth

Pritikin Split Pea Soup (salt)

Pritikin Minestrone Soup (cooked macaroni product)

Most of these soups are found in the health food section of the supermarket. It varies by store, however, and in many smaller markets you may not find them at all.

Canned Vegetables:

Green Giant Golden Sweet Corn—look for the "no salt or sugar added" on the package

Hunt's Whole Tomatoes (salt)

Progresso Crushed Tomatoes (salt)

It's very difficult to find any canned vegetable in regular supermarkets that isn't made with sugar—read labels.

Frozen Vegetables:

You'll have much better luck with frozen vegetables than with canned.

C & W frozen vegetables state right on the package that there is nothing added. The only exception might be salt. The same goes for Bird's Eye and Green Giant frozen vegetables. All freeze just the vegetables, occasionally with a trace of salt.

Tomato Pasta Sauces:

Contadina's Fresh Marinara Sauce (salt)

Enrico's Spaghetti Sauce

Enrico's Pasta Sauce

Romance's Fresh Marinara Sauce (salt)

Weight Watchers Spaghetti Sauce Flavored With Meat

Rice and Grains:

Pritikin Spanish Brown Rice

Frozen Soups:

Tabatchnick Soups

    Barley Bean

    Pea—look for the "no salt—no sugar added"

    Northern Bean

Unfortunately, virtually all frozen meals (Lean Cuisine, Weight Watchers, Swanson's, etc.) make dishes with cream sauces, wheat pasta, and other forbidden ingredients. You have no choice but to stay away from them, even though they'd make life a whole lot simpler.

If you're lucky enough to have a supermarket that has a "Special" or "Foreign" foods section, inspect it closely. Many of the items will be good for the most restrictive CFS diet. For instance, try substituting Chinese rice noodles or bean threads for pasta. In the Mexican cuisine arena, there are a multitude of beans and salsas that might work, and Middle Eastern delicacies such as tahini, sesame butter, and eggplant dip are delicious and also free of bad ingredients.

One final note: Any CFS sufferer needs pain relievers. Here, too, you must read labels carefully. Regular and Extra-Strength Tylenol are good, but the gel caps contain dyes. Excedrin Extra Strength contains 65 milligrams of caffeine per tablet. The shell around Advil contains sucrose and Nuprin has dyes in its products. You may have to choose between the lesser of many evils.

HEALTH FOOD STORES

You'll have a higher shopping batting average in health food stores. They tend to be more expensive, but there is a larger variety of acceptable foods. Also, the fruits and vegetables are more likely to be organically grown and pesticide-free.

The following is a list of foods that will work for the CFS diet. Once again, this is not an all-inclusive list, but it will get you started.

Even though the health food store products are generally better, you must still be vigilant. There are brands with some products that will work for you and others that won't.

In health food stores, some of the brands are regional, meaning that what may be readily available to us in Southern California (our local health food market is Mrs. Gooch) may not make its way to the upper expanses of Maine. Look for your own regional brands for some different and refreshing taste treats. However, the consumer demand for good food in the last decade has resulted in a dizzying array of delicious, nutritious national products. Many are listed here.

For your convenience we have marked the national brands with an *N* and the regional brands (our region being Southern California) with an *R*.

Bottled Juices:

Hienke's (N)
  100% Cranberry
  Juice—look
  for the
  "unsweetened"

L & A
  Pineapple Coconut

Freshly-Squeezed Juices:

Amazke (N)
  Almond Shake
  Mocha-Java
  Original Flavor
    Shake
  Vanilla Pecan Shake
Chiquita (N)
  Papaya Smoothie
  Protein Pump
Ferraro's Juices (R)
  Fresh Garden
    Vegetable
  Green Mix
  Lime
  Papaya Coconut
    Crème
  Pineapple Coconut
  Pineapple Mango
  Pineapple Papaya
  Protein Colada

  Salad in a Bottle
  Tropical Treat
  Veg-O-Green
  Veg-O-Mato
Hansen's (R)
  Coconut Juice
  Protein Pick-Up
Mighty Soy (R)
  Original
Naked Foods Juices (R)
  Carrot, Parsley, and
    Spinach
  Papaya and
    Pineapple
  Organic Carrot
  Carrot and Beet
Rice Dream (N)
  Organic Original
  Vanilla Lite

Milk:

    Meyenberg Goat's Milk (N)

Yogurt:

    Mystic Lake Dairy (N)   Redwood Hill Farm (N)

        Goat's Milk Plain   Goat's Milk Plain Yogurt
           Yogurt

Cheese:

    Alta-Dena (N)   Sonnet Farms (N)

        Goat Milk Cheese   Goat Milk Monterey
                        Jack

Butters:

    Hain (N)   Westbrae Natural (N)

        Almond Butter   Raw Cashew Butter

    Roaster Fresh   Roasted Cashew Butter

        Almond Butter   Smooth Almond Butter

        Cashew Butter

        Sunflower Butter

These butters spread on a rice cake with normal butter make a great instant snack.

Ready-Made Salads:

    Spa Salads (R)   Garlic Brown Rice

        Broccoli Corn Bean   Steamed Brown Rice

        Brown Rice Sauté   Steamed Brown Rice and

        Daily Greens with   Vegetables
           Lemon Pesto   7 Grain

Chips:

Blue Corn (N)
  Bearitos
Barbara's (N)
  Pinta Chips
Garden of Eatin' (N)
  Blue Chips—look
    for the "no salt
    added"
  Sesame Blues
Sunny Blues
  Yankee Doodles
Lapidus (N)
  Lite Corn—look for
    the "oil-free" Popcorn
Skinny (N)
  Natural Corn Chips—
    look for the "no salt"

Snacks:

Edward and Sons (N)
  Onion-Garlic Brown
    Rice Snaps
  Sesame Baked
    Brown Rice Snaps
Hol-Grain (N)
  Brown Rice Lite
    Snack Thins
Lundberg (N)
  Organic Brown Rice
    Mini Rice
    Cakes
  Organic Rice Cakes
  Organic Rice
    Cakes—Brown
    Rice
Organic Rice
    Cakes—Mochi
    Sweet
Organic Rice
    Cakes—Popcorn
Organic Rice
    Cakes—Wild Rice
Premier Japan (N)
  No Salt Sesame Rice
    Sembei Crackers
Pritikin (N)
  Rice Cakes—Multi-
    Grain
  Rice Cakes—Sesame

Snacks and Miscellaneous:

Buonapasta (R)
   Fresh Marinara
      Sauce
   Garlic Butter
Cedarlane (R)
   Eggplant Caviar

Hummus
Potato Salad
Judith's Natural Deli (R)
Hummus

Salsas and Dips:

Scotty's (R)
   Cajun Style
      Guacamole (salt)
   Fresh Salsa, Chunky
      Style (salt)
   Fresh Salsa, Herbs
      and Spices (salt)

Fresh Salsa,
   Tomatillos (salt)
Senor Felix's (R)
Salsa—Mild
Salsa—Medium Hot

Pasta:

Ancient Harvest (N)
   Quinoa Pasta
Cleopatra Amaranth
Pasta (N)
   Kamut Pasta
De Boles (N)
   Corn Pasta Elbows
   Corn Pasta
      Spaghetti
Mrs. Leeper's (N)
   Rice Pasta

Orgran (N)
   Barley and Spinach
      Pasta
   Corn Pasta
Pastariso (N)
   100% Rice Pasta
      Elbows
   100% Rice Pasta
      Spaghetti Style
Vita-Spelt (N)
   Whole Spelt Pasta

Tomato Sauces:

Enrico's (N)
    Traditional Sauce
Hagerty Foods (N)
    Artichoke Pasta
    Sauce

Mama Cocco's (N)
    Marinara Sauce

Dehydrated Soups:

Taste Adventure (N)
    Black Bean Chili
    Curry Lentil
    Lentil Chili

    Red Bean Chili
    Split Pea Soup
The Spice Hunter (N)
    Brown and Wild
        Rice Almondine

Canned Soups:

Hain (N)
    Turkey Rice Soup
    Vegetarian Chicken
        Broth (salt)
    Vegetarian Chicken
        Soup (salt)
    99% Fat-Free
        Vegetarian Split
        Pea Soup
    99% Fat-Free
        Vegetarian
        Lentil Soup
Health Valley (N)
    5 Bean Vegetable
        Soup
    Manhattan Clam
        Chowder

Pritikin (N)
    Chicken Broth
    Chicken Gumbo
    Lentil Soup
    Navy Bean Soup
    Split Pea Soup
Shelton's
    Black Bean and
        Chicken Soup
    Chicken Broth
    Chicken Chili
    Turkey Chili
    Turkey Rice Soup
    Vegetable Chicken
        Soup

Grain Dishes:

Ancient Harvest (N)
    Quinoa
Arrowhead Mills (N)
    Blue Cornmeal
    Quick Brown Rice
    Whole Grain Teff

Jerusalem Falafel
    Vegetable Burger
    Mix
Lundberg (N)
    Rizcous

Usually in this section of the health food store you will find a wonderful variety of nonwheat flours. Experiment and find what suits your taste the best. I personally enjoy the rice flours, but why limit yourself when you can try any or all of the following: soy flour, oat flour, cornmeal, brown rice flour, buckwheat flour, millet flour, teff flour, and amaranth flour.

Cereals:

Arrowhead Mills (N)
    Barley Flakes
    Bits O Barley
    Nature Puffs
    Nature O's
    Oat Bran
    Puffed Corn
    Puffed Millet
    Puffed Rice
Bob's Red Mill (N)
    8 Grain Wheatless
    Hot Cereal
Breadshop (N)
    Triple Bran

Ener G (N)
    Pure Rice Bran
Erewhon (N)
    Brown Rice Cream
    Oat Bran
Lundberg (N)
    Creamy Rice
Pocono (N)
    Cream of Buckwheat
Quick 'N Creamy (N)
    Brown Rice Hot
    Cereal
Tattorie Pandea
    Instant Polenta

Frozen Vegetables:

Cascadian Farm (N)
- Broccoli Cuts
- Corn
- Cut Green Beans
- French Fries
- Gardener's Blend
- Petits Pois (trace of salt)
- Sliced Carrots

C & W (N)
- Chopped Spinach
- French Cut Beans

- Petite Peas—look for the "no salt" added
- Petite Sweet Corn—look for the "sodium free"
- Whole Baby Carrots
- Whole Italian Green Beans

Health Valley (N)
- Leaf Spinach
- Whole Kernel Corn

Frozen Foods:

Amy's (N)
- Mexican Tamale Pies

Dos Banderos (R)
- Chicken Tamales

Jacyln's (N)
- Split Pea Soup

Mudpie (N)
- Veggie Burgers

Natural Touch (N)
- Lentil Rice Loaf

Tai (N)
- Channa Masala: chick peas
- Raj Mah: kidney beans

Tumaro's (N)
- Black Bean Enchiladas
- 2 Bean Tamales

PART TWO

The Phase One Diet

～ 4 ～

Mary's Quickies

O n your worst days, when you can't imagine cooking or shopping, have this stuff around to get you through the day.

੨෧

POPCORN

Healthy, tasty, and on-target for your diet. And easy—get the microwave kind, if you have a microwave, or the stovetop kind if you don't. Do check ingredient lists to be sure they haven't put forbidden ingredients such as cheese in.

੨෧

NUTS

Other than peanuts and pistaschios, you can eat all nuts. Have you savored a roasted cashew lately? Nuts can become your candy substitute. Unfortunately, like candy, nuts pack a lot of calories, so keep that in mind. Also, they can be hard to digest.

🐌

NUT BUTTER ON RICE CAKES

Again with the exception of peanuts and pistachios, nut butters are on the okay list. They're delicious on rice cakes. Top off with sliced bananas, if you're eating fruit, or if you're not, a layer of homemade mayonnaise.

🐌

WARMING "TEA"

1 cup hot water
1/4 tsp concentrated
   Vitamin C powder
   (found in health food
   stores)

A squeeze of lemon or
   lime, or add a dry
   parsley leaf — it
   cleanses the bladder

Mix in mug. This is nice in the morning, or before bed.

1 serving

🐌

"QUICKIE SALAD"

2 fresh tomatoes, sliced
Fresh basil

Extra-virgin olive oil
1/2 tsp lemon juice

On serving plates, alternate pieces of tomatoes and basil around the outside of the plate until a semicircle is formed. Drizzle with olive oil and lemon juice. Serve.

2 servings

ᨑ

QUICK STIR-FRY

This fast meal is all about exploiting whatever you have available. Stir fry rice, vegetables, and whatever unfinished, frozen dinner portions are kicking around your freezer. If you're using tomatoes, add them last and cook for only 30 seconds, so they don't fall apart. Eat wrapped up in tortillas, or just on a plate.

1 Tbs olive oil
Cooked rice

Leftovers — whatever's in the vegetable tray or freezer

Heat oil in a wok or medium-sized skillet. Add rice and all other ingredients. Cook for 3–4 minutes, stirring constantly until all vegetables are tender. A little bit of sesame oil and lemon juice add nice flavor notes to this simple meal.

Possible ingredients:
Onion
Tomatoes
Tuna fish, packed in water or oil
Celery
Broccoli
Dry roasted nuts
Any leftover fish, chicken, or meat

✏ 5 ✏

Breakfast

We usually think of breakfast dishes as cereal, pancakes, and sausage. Thinking like this will make you nuts if you're attempting to follow the CFS diet: Milk is not allowed, maple syrup is even more not allowed, and sausage is full of chemicals and sugar. Still, everybody needs a good, filling start to the day. So, be adventurous and stray from the beaten path. A pasta or rice dish can be a wonderful, sustaining substitute for usual breakfast fare. You'll find a number of wonderful pasta and rice dishes scattered about this book. Try them for breakfast.

Some good news—eggs are allowed! Fried eggs, scrambled eggs, poached eggs, hard-boiled eggs, eggs over easy, omelets—the list goes on. Now we know the cholesterol in eggs is a nutritional bugaboo in some quarters these days. Our attitude is that unless you know you have some real problem with cholesterol, be good to yourself by not worrying unduly about eggs. Since you're allowed to have them, have them without guilt. Enjoy!

Try one or more of the following, sautéed in oil, with scrambled eggs: chopped onions, chopped tomatoes, chopped bell peppers; or herbs such as parsley, chives, chervil, or tarragon. A garnish of caviar is fun. A side of salsa tastes and looks great with eggs. Eggs can be served on or with hot, buttered corn tortillas. Bacon is out—like sausage, it's usually made with sugar.

Other side dishes include broiled tomatoes and vegetables.

Here are some recipes we enjoy at breakfast:

❧

RICE CEREAL WITH CINNAMON

I said, "Mary, this isn't a recipe—it's cereal with cinnamon." She said, "I made it up, I cooked it—it's a recipe." So here it is: Rice Cereal With Cinnamon.

This is simplicity itself, and quite delicious. Find a packaged rice cereal with no bad ingredients, which is made from whole, unrefined rice. Cereal should cook with water.

Packaged whole rice cereal   Butter
Cinnamon

Prepare cereal according to package directions. Add cinnamon and butter to taste.

1 serving

🐌

HOMINY GRITS

Hominy is kernels of hulled dried corn with the germ removed. Grind them, and you have hominy grits. The following recipe is the basic preparation for this popular Southern breakfast dish. If you buy your grits packaged, just follow the directions on the box. (Note: Packaged grits are much faster and easier to make.)

I have never been a great fan of grits, or "gareeyuts" as they say in the South. But for a filling, fast breakfast, they do the trick. When I eat them, I splurge on the butter and add any flavor element that's handy: pine nuts, cinnamon, even onion. Grits take on the personality of whatever's available, so think of them as a blank culinary canvas and be creative.

1 cup grits	1 tsp salt
Water	Butter (optional)

Soak grits in water to cover 1 hour. Drain. Add 3 cups boiling water and salt. Cook gently for up to 1 hour. Cooking time varies depending on whether grits are ground fine, medium, or coarse. When grits are tender, they are done. Beat butter into hot grits if desired, and serve.

2 servings

❧

MEXICAN BEANS

Beans for breakfast? Sure. They make a good accompaniment to Huevos Rancheros (pg. 43), or even plain old fried eggs, taking the place of toast. One of the upsides of this diet is that you get some relief from the boredom of having the same things for breakfast, day in, day out—toast, cereal, coffee...

2 garlic cloves, diced   1 29-oz can pinto beans
2 Tbs olive oil

Heat the olive oil in a skillet. Add the garlic and cook gently for about 2–3 minutes — don't let it burn. Gradually stir in the liquid from the beans until the mixture thickens. Finally, add the beans. Mash half the beans and cook until everything is blended.

4 servings

❧

BREAKFAST BURRITOS

Throw whatever's on hand into this one—chopped cilantro, pimento, green onion...This is a good, hearty, healthy breakfast, but could use some flavor excitement. In the herb and spice section of your market, there's something called "Mexican Seasoning" which you can add while sautéing that'll bring some additional character to the dish. Also try fresh salsas.

1 8-oz can refried beans
1/2 cup cooked brown rice
1/2 cup ground turkey
1 red pepper, diced

1 small onion, chopped
4–6 corn tortillas
1 tsp butter

Combine beans, rice, turkey, pepper, and onion and sauté 5 minutes.

Butter tortillas and zap in microwave. Or wrap in foil and heat 5 minutes in oven or toaster-oven.

Wrap tortillas around bean mix and serve hot.

4 servings

❧

BURRITOS WITH SCRAMBLED EGGS

One of the good things about moving to Southern California (Mary's from Wisconsin, I'm from New York) was all the Mexican food we found here. It always seems not only to taste good but be extremely wholesome and healthy as well. If chicken soup is "Jewish penicillin," maybe these breakfast burritos are "Hispanic erythromycin."

1 small onion, minced	1 medium tomato, diced
1 garlic clove, minced	7 eggs, beaten
2 Tbs butter	Warm corn tortillas
2 zucchini, diced	Salsa (if desired)
1/2 green pepper, diced	Cilantro leaves

Sauté onion and garlic in butter until onion is soft, about 5 minutes. Add the zucchini, pepper, and tomato and cook until the zucchini is tender. Stir until liquid evaporates. Pour in the eggs and scramble until the eggs are set.

Spoon egg mixture into warmed tortillas. Top with salsa. Garnish with cilantro leaves.

6 servings

🐚

HUEVOS RANCHEROS

Hey, more Mexican. This recipe is simple as can be, and absolutely delicious. It's one of our favorite breakfasts—very festive.

1 garlic clove, minced
1 onion, chopped
3 Tbs butter
1 pimento, chopped

3 tomatoes, chopped
8 eggs
8 corn tortillas

Cook garlic and onion in 2 tablespoons butter until lightly browned. Add pimento and tomatoes. Simmer until thickened. In a separate pan, cook eggs sunny side up in remaining butter. Place each egg on a warmed tortilla and pour sauce over.

4 servings

❧

EGGS BENEDICT

The challenge here is poaching the eggs so that they hold together. The usual way this is done is by adding a bit of vinegar to the water. If you're not allergic to vinegar, we recommend this approach. If you don't want to add vinegar, try putting each egg in a shallow cup, like a Japanese teacup, then upending it into the simmering water. Actually leave the cup in the water for 30 seconds or so, then remove. This can help hold the egg together, too. But vinegar is easier.

Water	4 rice cakes
8 eggs	Hollandaise sauce (see
Butter	Chapter 8.)

In a large skillet, simmer an inch of water. Add the eggs one at a time and poach 3–5 minutes.

Meanwhile, butter the rice cakes and set aside. Put 2 rice cakes on each plate.

Remove the eggs with slotted spoon and place on the rice cakes. Top with hollandaise.

4 servings

&

EGGS FLORENTINE

This recipe better be for one of your less tired mornings. Maybe you'll use it as a treat for New Year's or Labor Day—it takes a while. The good news is it's lusciously delicious and will leave you feeling so undeprived you won't crave forbidden ingredients for a week.

1 cup rice	4–8 eggs
1 small white onion, minced	4 cooked artichoke bottoms (get the kind that are marinated in water)
1 Tbs butter	
1 bunch spinach, well washed, trimmed, and chopped	
	Hollandaise sauce (see Chapter 8)
Pinch nutmeg	Dash paprika

Cook rice.

Sauté onion in butter. Add spinach and cook until soft, no more than 3 minutes. Add nutmeg, stir. Set aside and keep warm.

Poach eggs.

Put artichoke bottoms on hot plates, then spread with spinach mixture. Top each with one or two poached eggs. Add hollandaise sauce and a dash of paprika. Serve with heated rice.

4 servings

❧

FRENCH EGGS

This is a filling, festive, "special" recipe. You can probably find canned snails in your supermarket or specialty store—we were able to get ours at the local Ralphs. Certainly not for every day, it makes a nice surprise for, oh, Bob Dylan's birthday. By the way, this recipe's great without the snails, too.

1/2 lb canned snails, rinsed and drained	1/2 cup walnuts, chopped
3 garlic cloves, finely chopped	3 Tbs parsley, finely chopped
1/2 cup butter	12 eggs

Sauté the snails and garlic in 1/4 cup of butter over medium heat for 5 minutes. Remove from heat and stir in the walnuts and parsley.

Whisk the eggs in a large bowl until frothy. Melt the remaining butter in a large skillet. Add eggs. Cook over low heat for 2–3 minutes, stirring constantly, until eggs are set. Add the snail mixture and stir well. Remove from heat and serve.

6 servings

🕭

PIPERADE

This recipe goes back to the days when my carefree, twentysomething friends and I used to share a summer house on Fire Island. We concocted this as a good breakfast after a night of carousing. We called it "piperade" because it contained tomato and thyme, like the French dish, and because my friend Marylyn liked the word, either in its French pronunciation (peeper-odd) or in American (piper-ade, like a drink).

2 Tbs oil	1/2 tsp thyme
2 medium onions, sliced	7 Tbs butter
4 garlic cloves, minced	Corn tortillas
1/2 bay leaf	12 eggs, lightly beaten
2 large tomatoes, peeled and chopped	

Heat oil. Add onion, garlic, bay leaf, tomatoes, and thyme. Cook 15 minutes over low heat, stirring occasionally.

Meanwhile, melt butter in medium skillet and cook tortillas over low heat 2 minutes.

Add eggs to the onion mixture in the large skillet and cook, stirring over medium heat, until eggs thicken.

Put tortillas on warmed plates and cover with eggs.

6 servings

❧

GARLIC CORNMEAL CAKES

Eat these hot with plain or herb butter. Go ahead, slather it on—you've got enough dietary restrictions to worry about. Your kids, by the way, will enjoy these with pancake syrup.

1/4 cup butter	3 cups water
1 small onion, minced	1-1/4 cups cornmeal
1 garlic clove, diced	1 Tbs olive oil (optional)

Preheat oven to 325° F. Meanwhile heat butter in a large saucepan, add onion, and sauté until soft. Add garlic and sauté for 1 minute. Add 3 cups of water and bring to a boil. Add the cornmeal, stirring constantly.

Cover and transfer the pan to the oven. Cook 25–30 minutes and serve. Or if you like, brush each square with a bit of the olive oil, then grill or broil, turning once, until cornmeal cakes are browned slightly, about 5 minutes.

6 servings

🐚

SPINACH TOMATO FRITTATA

Dirt is not on your diet, so wash the spinach well, plunging it into a bowl of cold water and draining, and repeating this process until no more dirt comes away. Spinach, parsley, and leeks are the Pigpens of the vegetable world, always covered with dirt, so be sure to give them a bath before eating.

3 Tbs butter
1 lb spinach, all stems
    trimmed, rinsed
2 eggs, lightly beaten

1 tomato, seeded and
    diced
1 Tbs minced onion
1 tsp minced garlic
1/4 tsp nutmeg

Preheat oven to 375° F.

Melt butter in skillet. Stir in spinach and cook 4 minutes until wilted. Chop and place in a bowl.

Grease a 9-inch pie pan. Stir eggs, tomatoes, onion, garlic, and nutmeg into spinach. Spoon into the pie pan. Bake until batter sets, about 15 minutes.

Butter a baking sheet. Invert pie pan onto sheet, removing pie pan. Bake the frittata another 7–10 minutes until completely done. Cut into wedges and serve.

4 servings

&a

CORN CASSEROLE

You'll find all sorts of tricky ways to separate the yolks of eggs described in cookbooks. The easiest way is to break open the egg, empty it into your hand, and hold your fingers far enough apart to let the white run through, leaving the yolk in your hand. You can put a bowl underneath if you want to save the whites. You may, like me, find you quite enjoy the cold, slimy feel of the white against your fingers. Or you may not—there's a strong possibility I'm weird.

1/2 cup olive oil
1/2 cup onion, chopped
1-1/2 cups green peppers, finely chopped
1 large tomato, skinned and chopped

2 cups frozen corn kernels, unfrozen
2 egg yolks
2 hard-boiled eggs, chopped
1/4 tsp thyme

Preheat oven to 350° F. In a skillet, heat 1/4 cup of the oil and sauté 1/4 cup of the onion and 1 cup of the green peppers until onion is tender. Add the tomato and cook for 10 minutes. Then add the corn and egg yolks and cook, stirring, for an additional 3 minutes.

Heat the remaining oil in another skillet and sauté the remaining onion and green pepper until the onion is tender. Add the hard-boiled eggs and thyme and mix well.

Spread half the corn mixture in the bottom of a greased 1½-quart baking dish. Top with the hard-boiled egg mixture and then the remaining corn mixture. Bake about 15 minutes or until the corn is tender and the mixture is heated through.

4 servings

❧

MEXICAN STIR-FRY

I told Mary this is a great breakfast dish because it's so colorful it'll wake you up just looking at it. As a side benefit, it's delicious and healthily filling—it'll take you right through the morning.

1 Tbs olive oil
2 garlic cloves, minced
1 medium onion, minced
2 small zucchini, diced
1 large sweet red pepper, diced
1 15 1/2-oz can garbanzo beans, rinsed and drained

1 15-oz can black beans, rinsed and drained
1/2 cup water
1/4 tsp oregano
2 Tbs tomato puree
Warm corn tortillas
1/4 cup cilantro leaves, diced

Heat the olive oil in a wok or nonstick frying pan. Add the garlic, onions, zucchini, and red pepper. Stir-fry until the onions are tender, about 2 minutes. Add the garbanzo and black beans. Stir-fry an additional minute. Finally, add the water, oregano, and tomato puree. Stir-fry until hot, about 30 seconds.

Serve with the warm tortillas, garnish with cilantro.

4 servings

·ℰ·

BREAKFAST STIR-FRY

Another wonderfully filling meal. Include any intriguing leftovers you may have in the refrigerator. Eat wrapped in warmed corn tortillas, if you wish.

This probably takes longer to prepare than most breakfasts you're used to, but once it's cooked you have instant breakfast awaiting you for three additional days—a week if you live alone.

2 cups cooked rice, chilled	2 Tbs peanut oil
1 chicken breast, skinned, boned, and cut into 1/2-inch chunks	5 large green onions, thinly sliced
1 tsp fresh ginger, minced	2 carrots, minced
2 garlic cloves, minced	2 cups broccoli
1 Tbs water	1/2 cup chicken broth
2 tsp sesame oil	

Cook rice the night before and put in refrigerator. Mix chicken breast, ginger, garlic, water, and sesame oil together in a small bowl. Cover and also put in refrigerator.

In morning, heat 1 tablespoon of peanut oil in a wok or nonstick pan over high heat. When very hot, add rice and half the green onions. Stir-fry over high heat for 2 minutes. Set aside in a large bowl.

Heat remaining oil. Add carrots and broccoli. Stir-fry until heated through, about 2 minutes. Add chicken broth and boil while stirring for 2 minutes, until vegetables are just tender. Add to bowl.

Add chicken breast mixture to wok, stir-fry for a minute or two — the chicken cooks fast.

Pour contents of bowl back into wok. Stir-fry until well-mixed and heated through. Garnish with remaining green onions.

6–8 servings

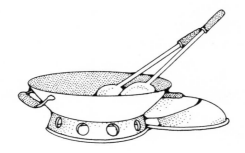

❧

STUFFED TOMATOES

5 large tomatoes
1-1/2 cups falafel mix

2 Tbs fresh parsley,
  chopped
1 Tbs olive oil

Preheat oven to 350° F.

Cut the tops off the tomatoes and scoop out the insides. Turn upside down on paper towels and drain. Cut the seeded pieces into cubes and set aside.

In a medium bowl, prepare the falafel mix according to directions. Stir in the tomato chunks and parsley.

Put the tomato shells in a shallow baking pan and stuff with the falafel mixture. Drizzle with olive oil. Bake for 15 minutes.

5 servings

❧

STUFFED PEPPERS

3 red peppers, cut in half
   and cleaned
1 small green pepper, cut
   in half and cleaned
4 Tbs oil
1/2 cup quick-cook rice
1 cup chicken broth

1/2 lb ground turkey
1 garlic clove, minced
3/4 cup onion
1 Tbs fresh or dried
   sage leaves, minced
2 Tbs pine nuts, toasted

Place the red and green peppers skin side up on a broiler pan and broil until skins are slightly browned in spots and flesh is tender. Set red peppers aside. Dice green pepper when cool.

Put 1 tablespoon oil in a hot skillet, add the rice, and sauté about 2 minutes. Add the chicken broth and bring to a boil. Reduce heat to a simmer, uncovered, and cook about 12 minutes until rice is cooked and liquid has been absorbed.

Meanwhile, sauté turkey in remaining oil, stirring constantly until meat loses its pink color. Add the diced pepper, garlic, and onion and continue cooking until turkey is cooked and vegetables are tender. Stir in the sage, pine nuts, and cooked rice. Heat thoroughly. Spoon mixture into red pepper halves.

6 servings

🛥

KASHA AND SWISS CHARD

For people who think they don't like vegetables, this sensual eating experience could change a lot of minds—it's that voluptuous and flavorsome. If this dish were an actress, it would be Greta Scacchi. If an actor, possibly Tom Berringer.

4 large red Swiss chard stalks, trimmed	1 cup chicken broth
4 Tbs butter	1/2 cup whole kasha (a.k.a. buckwheat groats)
1/2 medium onion, chopped	1 egg, lightly beaten

Cut chard leaves from ribs. Halve ribs lengthwise and slice thinly crosswise. Shred leaves. Melt 2 tablespoons butter in heavy medium saucepan. Add onion and chard ribs. Cook about 10 minutes over moderate heat, stirring occasionally, until onion is tender. Add shredded leaves. Cook another 5 minutes. Add broth and bring to boil.

Meanwhile, combine kasha and 1/2 of egg in bowl. Heat heavy large skillet. Add kasha mixture and stir until egg dries and kasha kernels separate, about 3 minutes. Reduce heat to low. Add broth and vegetable mixture. Simmer covered until kasha is tender and liquid is absorbed—about 20 minutes. Add remaining butter and toss well.

2 servings

⁊

CHIVE POLENTA WITH SUN-DRIED TOMATOES

If you can find a packaged precooked polenta without bad ingredients, it makes this a bit easier—you only have to stir for 5 minutes. Just use cornmeal instead. We like Fattorie and Pandea Instant Polenta, which is imported from Italy and sold at most health food stores.

Our friend Paula, who kitchen-tested this recipe for us, says she prefers the polenta plain, without the tomato paste. But Paula enjoys making provocative statements—you should hear her go on about Bruce Springsteen. Anyway, we leave your choice of how to serve this to your personal taste buds.

3 cups chicken broth	2 Tbs minced parsley
1-1/4 cup yellow cornmeal	3 Tbs butter
1/4 cup minced chives	Sun-dried tomato paste

Preheat broiler.

In a large, heavy, ovenproof pan, bring broth to boil. Gradually whisk in cornmeal. Cook, stirring often, until mixture pulls away from side of pan — about 15 minutes.

Whisk in chives, parsley, and 1 tablespoon butter. Dot top of polenta with additional butter.

Stick the pan under the broiler and broil polenta until lightly browned — about 2–4 minutes. Let stand 5 minutes. Cut in wedges, then cut wedges in half lengthwise, and spread with remaining butter and sun-dried tomato paste.

2–4 servings

🐟

SAUTÉED BROOK TROUT

Sure, fish for breakfast. Mary's dad lives in front of a lake, and sometimes gets up early to catch a few rockfish. Dipped in cornmeal and cooked up fast, nothing could taste better. And if you don't live in front of a lake, the trout you can get at your supermarket will do fine.

2–4 trouts, cleaned   2 Tbs butter
1/2 cup cornmeal

Choose the smallest, freshest fish available. Dip in cornmeal to coat. Sauté in butter until browned on both sides. Serve immediately.

2 servings

❦ 6 ❧

Lunch

Three possibilities here: away from home, home but tired, home and not so tired.

Away from home, pack some of Mary's quickies, or use restaurants that have suitable foods—Middle Eastern, Mexican, or seafood. If you're at home or packing a lunch, read on for some delicious and not-too-taxing recipes.

SANDWICHES

The following recipes are the ones you should try when you are "home but tired." These sandwiches aren't exactly like the ones you get at the deli, but they taste delicious and don't take much time or energy to prepare.

Eat bread only if you're not allergic to anything in it: yeast, wheat, whatever. If you're not eating bread, corn tortillas are fine, wheat ones okay if you're allowed wheat. Rice cakes (made from whole grain unprocessed rice) are fine, too, assuming they don't have cheese or some other no-no worked into them.

✌

CHICKEN SALAD SANDWICH

When I was a kid, all I ever had for lunch were three kinds of sandwiches: chicken salad, tuna salad, and peanut butter and jelly. How nice that two of them are still fine to eat, despite the diet. And I find that they still taste great, even unaccompanied by chocolate milk.

1 cooked chicken from
    supermarket, skinned
    and chopped
1/2 cup celery, chopped

3/4 cup homemade may-
    onnaise (see Chapter
    8)

Toss all ingredients in a bowl and spread on rice cakes or wrap up in tortillas.

6 servings

(Try with curry powder, lemon juice, and chopped basil leaves. Or tarragon, chopped cucumber, and chopped water chestnuts or walnuts.)

🐟

TUNA SALAD SANDWICH

1 small can tuna (6-1/8 oz)
1/4 cup homemade mayon-
    naise, more to taste
    (see Chapter 8)

1/4 cup purple onion,
    diced
Butter
6 rice cakes
1/4 cup fresh parsley,
    chopped

Combine tuna, mayonnaise, and onion. Mix well. Butter rice cakes. Top with tuna mixture. Garnish with parsley.

2 servings

(Variations — add one or more of the following ingredients: chopped coriander, chopped celery, curry powder, lemon juice, tomato slices, basil.)

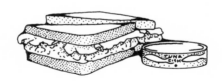

🐌

EGG SALAD WITH CUMIN

Egg salad sandwiches I didn't have as a kid. That was because I didn't think I liked egg salad. All these years later, with this recipe, I've discovered that I do like it. So I guess the moral is, kids don't know what they like. Anyway, this recipe I bet you'll like.

1/3 cup homemade mayonnaise (see Chapter 8)	6 hard-boiled eggs, chopped
1 Tbs lemon juice	1/2 cup diced celery
3/4 tsp ground cumin	1/4 cup thinly sliced green onions

Mix all ingredients together in bowl until well combined. Spread on rice cakes or wrap up in heated tortillas.

Makes about two cups.

4 servings

👈

OTHER SANDWICH IDEAS

Grilled chicken breast with tarragon mayonnaise

Chopped shrimp with mayonnaise

Chopped lobster with mayonnaise

Hard-boiled egg, tuna, and mayonnaise

Sautéed eggplant with mayonnaise

Crabmeat with lemon juice and chives

Hard-boiled egg, onion, and mayonnaise

Hard-boiled egg, onion, raw spinach, and mayonnaise

These dishes take a little longer, but all are good and on-target for your diet when you are "Home and Less Tired." Though we have arbitrarily put them into the "Lunch" chapter, they of course taste just as good for dinner, for breakfast, or for midnight snacks. Lentil soup, for example, on a chilly morning, makes as good a breakfast as you could possibly imagine.

Soups

❧

BEAN SOUP

4 cups chicken broth
1/2 cup carrots, sliced
1/2 cup onion, sliced
2 Tbs lemon juice

3 cups white beans, cooked and drained, or canned white beans

Combine broth, carrots, onion, and lemon juice in a saucepan. Simmer, covered, until carrots are just tender. Stir in beans. Heat thoroughly.

4 servings

🍂

TIM'S BUTTERNUT SQUASH SOUP

This is a lush, velvety experience, a soup that's voluptuous. If serving wine to guests, try a sweet one. In fact, try Quady Essencia—the combination should be an eye-opener.

The soup was invented by my old pal Tim back in those Fire Island house days. We depended on Tim to keep us fed no matter what madness was going on, and he always had a pot of something warm and nourishing on the stove. Thanks, pal.

2 Tbs butter
2 Tbs vegetable oil
2 cups onion, chopped
1/2 cup water
6 cups chicken broth

3 1/2-lb butternut squash, peeled, halved, and seeded, then cut into 1/2-inch cubes

Heat butter and oil in a large skillet, add onion, and cook at low heat until soft, about 8 minutes. Add squash and 1/2 cup of water. Cook, covered, over moderately low heat for 30 minutes, until squash is tender. Add chicken broth and simmer uncovered for 15 minutes.

Process the soup in a blender or food processor by batches.

8 servings

Note: Soup may be made in advance and kept chilled in the refrigerator.

🐌

LENTIL SOUP

This humble lentil soup is great on chilly nights. All you need for accompaniment is a simple salad and some heated corn tortillas with butter. For those without CFS, substitute crusty bread for the tortillas. It's one of those dinners that tastes so healthy you think it'll cure you all by itself. It probably won't, but it sure won't hurt.

1 cup lentils
3 cups water
1 carrot, diced
2/3 cup onion, chopped
1 bay leaf
1/8 tsp ground thyme

2 Tbs butter
1 lb tomatoes, chopped and seeded, or, on your low-energy days, 1 (16-oz) can whole tomatoes, drained and chopped

Rinse lentils. Place in a pot with water, carrot, onion, bay leaf, and thyme. Bring to a boil over medium heat. Cover and simmer over low heat for 45 minutes. Add butter and tomatoes. Heat through. Serve.

4 servings

🏵

TOMATO-GARLIC SOUP

Peeling and seeding tomatoes doesn't have to be all that hard. Just heat a large pot of water to boiling, turn off heat, and drop tomatoes in for 1 minute. Then pour tomatoes into a colander and spray with cold water to stop the cooking process. Now cut tomatoes in half and squeeze over sink. The seeds pop out and the skin pulls off easily. You are now ready for chopping.

With Italian plum tomatoes, you need to let them soak 2 minutes—their skins are tighter or something.

4 medium garlic cloves,
    peeled and minced
2 Tbs olive oil
2 lbs Italian plum
    tomatoes, peeled,
    seeded, and chopped

1-1/4 qts chicken broth
6 basil leaves, chopped

In a large pot, sauté garlic in the olive oil over low to moderate heat. Add the tomatoes and cook over low heat, uncovered, for about 10 minutes, stirring frequently.

Add the chicken broth and simmer for 20 minutes.

Stir in basil and serve. Or chill and serve, adding basil as garnish.

4 servings

🛥

GAZPACHO

Yet another recipe from Fire Island. We were always having so much fun out there that we had to eat as healthily as possible to compensate for the havoc we were wreaking on ourselves. I guess this worked, since we're all still around today.

1 carrot, peeled
1/4 red onion
2 green onions, each cut
    into several pieces
2 cucumbers, peeled,
    seeded, and cut in
    chunks

Juice of 1/2 lime
3 pts cherry tomatoes
Chives, chopped

Puree carrot, red and green onions, cucumbers, and lime juice in the food processer or blender. Add tomatoes and puree until gazpacho is the consistency of soup.

Chill. Serve in soup bowls garnished with chopped chives.

6 servings

🐚

SPECIAL CHICKEN SOUP

A fine chicken soup. Nuff said.

6 cups chicken broth
2 lbs boned chicken meat,
    trimmed and cut into
    pieces
1/3 cup cooked nonwheat
    pasta

Juice of 1 lemon or lime
2 eggs
1/2 cup coriander,
    minced

Heat broth and add chicken pieces. Simmer until meat is cooked, about 5 minutes. Add the pasta, bring to a simmer, and remove from heat.

Squeeze 3 tablespoons of the lime or lemon juice into a bowl. Add the eggs and whisk together. Gradually add 2 cups of the broth to the egg mixture, whisking constantly. Slowly whisk the eggs into the soup mixture.

Return to low heat until soup starts to steam. Add coriander and serve at once.

4 servings

&.

CARROT SOUP

Names of food items can be misleading. Here, this lush concoction, fit for kings and movie stars, is given the simple cognomen "Carrot Soup." Try it—we're not talking Campbell's. In fact, our friend Paula, who did try it, thought it was the best carrot soup she ever had—or imagined.

1 medium onion, sliced very thin
2 Tbs unsalted butter
8 medium carrots, peeled and sliced 1/4 inch thick

2 cups chicken broth
1 Tbs peeled fresh gingerroot, finely minced
1 Tbs fresh thyme leaves

In a large saucepan cook the onion in the butter until soft. Add the carrots and broth and simmer, covered, for 20 minutes.

Puree carrots in batches in a food processor or blender. Transfer the puree to the saucepan, add the gingerroot and thyme, and simmer, stirring for 10 minutes.

4 servings

❧

COLD AVOCADO SOUP

The key element here is lime juice. I've always been deeply impressed with limes—their color, their perfume, their fantastic flavor. As far as I'm concerned, you can forget your fancy theological arguments—limes alone are sufficient proof of the existence of God. For this recipe, any lime will do, but get key limes if you can. They're sweeter.

4 avocados, mashed	4 cups chicken broth
Juice of 2 limes	8 lime slices

Place mashed avocado and lime juice in food processor or blender, add some of the chicken broth and blend. Continue blending while adding the rest of the chicken broth until mixture is smooth and easy to pour. Add more lime juice to taste.

Chill soup. Garnish with lime slices when ready to serve.

8 servings

⠦

AVGOLEMONO SOUP

This seems to be the national soup of Greece. It's seriously delicious. Isn't it great that we can give you great-tasting recipes like this so that you don't have to eat, I don't know, wheat germ and mashed tofu or something?

5 cups chicken broth
1 cup water
1/4 cup instant rice
1/4 cup fresh lemon juice
3 eggs

1/2 lb cooked chicken, diced
2 Tbs fresh dill, chopped (optional)

In a saucepan combine all of the chicken broth and 1 cup of water and bring to a boil. Stir in rice and cook according to directions on box.

In a separate bowl whisk together the lemon juice and eggs, and whisk in 1 cup of the broth until fully mixed. Then whisk this back into the remaining broth. Add the chicken and cook over medium-low heat, whisking, for 3 minutes. Do not allow to boil.

Serve and garnish with the dill if desired.

6 servings

🕭

ONION SOUP

This is not the cheesy French onion soup, but a light, refreshing, and colorful American one. Makes a nice lunch or first course.

1 yellow bell pepper, cored, seeded, and cut into thin strips	1 onion, diced
	1-1/2 tsp fresh thyme
	3 cups chicken broth
3 Tbs butter	1 small tomato, peeled,
2 leeks, trimmed, quartered lengthwise, and cut into 1/2-inch pieces	seeded, and diced

In 1 tablespoon of butter, sauté pepper over low heat, about 20 minutes.

Meanwhile, heat the remaining butter in a large pot over medium-low heat. Add the leeks and cook for 3 minutes. Add the onion and cook, stirring frequently, until soft, about 10 minutes. Stir in the thyme. Add the broth, bring to boil, and simmer for 5 minutes.

Add the tomato and bell pepper to the soup and cook over low heat until just heated through.

4 servings

Salads

🕿

SHRIMP AND CORN SALAD

This is great summer eating. Serve in a big lettuce leaf. Or in an avocado. Heck, serve it in your bowling ball bag—it tastes great anywhere.

2 cups frozen corn kernels
1/2 lb small cooked shrimp
1 cup chopped celery
3 green onions, chopped

1/4 tsp curry powder
1/2 cup homemade mayonnaise (see Chapter 8)

Cook corn according to package directions. Add the shrimp and the remaining ingredients to the corn and stir well. Refrigerate for at least 1 hour before serving.

4 servings

🐌

CALIFORNIA SALAD

If you like the sort of food where sweet juicy things explode in your mouth, this recipe is for you. You can substitute red cherry tomatoes for the yellow ones. You can substitute lime juice for lemon juice. Just don't substitute regular onions for the red ones, or they'll be calling you Flame-breath for the rest of the night.

1 lb red tomatoes, cut into wedges	1/2 cup fresh basil leaves
1/2 lb yellow cherry tomatoes, stems removed	1/2 red onion, chopped
	1/4 cup extra-virgin olive oil
	2 Tbs lemon juice

In a large bowl combine tomatoes, basil, onion, and oil, and toss well. Add lemon juice and toss again.

4 servings

🍂

SQUID SALAD

1/3 cup lemon juice
1 Tbs lemon peel, grated
1-1/4 cup light olive oil
1-1/4 lbs squid, cleaned
    and cut into rings

3 celery stalks, chopped
2 medium red bell pep-
    pers, quartered and
    cut into strips
2 Tbs fresh basil,
    chopped

In a small bowl combine the lemon juice and peel, and gradually whisk in 3/4 cup of olive oil.

In a large skillet, heat 3 tablespoons of olive oil over high heat. Add the squid and tentacles and stir-fry until opaque, about 1-1/2 minutes. Transfer the squid to a colander. Add the remaining 2 tablespoons of olive oil to the skillet and reheat. Cook the celery, stirring until tender, about 2 minutes. Using a slotted spoon, add the celery to the squid. Next stir-fry the peppers until just soft, about 1 minute.

Return the squid and celery to the skillet. Add the basil and stir-fry until just heated through. Put the mixture in a new bowl and add the dressing. Chill.

4 servings

❧

SEAFOOD SALAD

This is a fresh, delicious meal that's just right on a hot day. The prep work is a bit labor-intensive—save time by buying the shrimp already cooked, and not bothering to skin the tomatoes. We won't tell.

1/2 lb bay scallops
1/2 cup lime juice
3 dozen medium shrimp, cooked
2 medium tomatoes, chopped
1 onion, finely chopped

1 large avocado, peeled and cubed
3 Tbs cilantro, finely chopped
6 large lettuce leaves (optional)

Put the scallops and lime juice in a large glass bowl. Marinate in the refrigerator for an hour. (The lime juice will "cook" the scallops.) Then add all other ingredients. Toss and serve in lettuce leaves if you wish.

6 servings

❧

EGGPLANT PASTA SALAD

This works two ways—warm as a pasta side dish, or cold as a salad, which was especially nice on the 100° + day we most recently cooked it.

5 Tbs olive oil

4 Japanese eggplants cut in 1/4-inch slices

1 red pepper, cut into thin strips

1 yellow pepper, cut into thin strips

1/2 small red onion, cut into thin strips

1 medium garlic clove, crushed

1/2 cup basil leaves, chopped

1 pkg (8 oz) cooked quinoa pasta shells

3 Tbs fresh lemon juice

1/4 cup pine nuts, toasted

1 bunch arugula, chopped

In a large skillet, heat 2 tablespoons of olive oil over medium heat. Cook the eggplant in batches until browned on both sides, adding more oil if necessary. Remove the eggplant when cooked to large bowl.

When all the eggplant is cooked, add the remaining olive oil to the skillet and sauté the peppers and onion until soft, about 5 minutes. Add the garlic and basil, and cook an additional 5 minutes.

Add the pepper mixture, pasta, lemon juice, pine nuts, and arugula to the eggplant bowl and toss well.

6 servings

🐌

BARLEY-CORN SALAD

Man, have we ever learned about grains since we got on this diet. I don't know about you, but for us, barley was something that just never came up. The best thing I could think of to say about barley was that it rhymed with Marley, as in Bob, my favorite singer of all time. But barley, like so many of these exotic food items we've learned about, turns out to be soulful and delicious, and this is an extra-good salad. Give it a shot.

1 cup barley, rinsed well
    and drained
1 cup red bell pepper,
    chopped
1-1/2 cups corn kernels

1/2 cup fresh parsley
    leaves, chopped
2 Tbs lemon juice
1/3 cup olive oil

In a large saucepan of boiling water, slowly add barley and boil, stirring and skimming the froth for 30 minutes, or until barley is tender. Drain, rinse with cold water, and cool.

Transfer the barley to a large bowl and add pepper, corn, and parsley. In a small bowl mix lemon juice and oil, adding more lemon juice or oil depending on your taste. Toss salad with dressing.

6 servings

🍃

BLACK BEAN SALAD

We've learned to love black beans. In addition to this good salad, you can eat them just warmed up with maybe a little chopped onion, and some rice on the side. Mary serves them that way with mussels, which our six-year-old unaccountably loves.

3 Tbs lemon juice

1/3 cup olive oil

16-oz can of black beans, liquid discarded, blanched in boiling water for 5 seconds, and drained

1 cup onion, chopped

2 Tbs sun-dried tomatoes, minced

2 cups romaine lettuce, rinsed, shredded, and chilled

In a bowl, add the lemon juice and then slowly add the oil, whisking until dressing is emulsified. Add beans, onion, and tomatoes and toss well.

Divide romaine lettuce onto 4 plates. Top with bean salad and serve.

2 servings

Seafood

Seafood is such a wonderful food. You can dress it up or down, and the possibilities are endless. For an easy lunch simply pan-fry or grill some fish; if you care for something a little more exciting—try these.

🐌

SWORDFISH CEVICHE

Good eatin' for hot weather—you don't have to heat up the kitchen.

8 oz swordfish or other
fish steak, cut into 1/4-
inch cubes
1/3 cup fresh lime juice
2 medium tomatoes,
peeled, seeded, and
diced
1/2 cup tomato juice

3 Tbs olive oil
3 Tbs fresh oregano,
coarsely chopped
1/2 bay leaf

Put swordfish in a large bowl, toss with lime juice, and marinate in the refrigerator for 1 hour. Drain swordfish and return to bowl. Add all remaining ingredients and toss well. Cover and refrigerate for at least 1 more hour.

4 servings

❧

RATATOUILLE WITH SHRIMP

This is a more labor-intensive recipe than most. That's the bad news. The good is that it's unbelievably delicious and falls within the parameters of your diet.

A long, slow cooking process brings out unbelievable flavors in the vegetables. Remember, you'll need to start early. This is probably a Saturday meal rather than a Wednesday one.

1 large yellow onion, cut into 1/2-inch-thick slices

1/2 lb eggplant, cut into 1/2-inch-thick slices

1/2 lb zucchini, cut into 1/2-inch-thick slices

2 garlic cloves

2 green peppers, seeded and cut in strips

1 lb tomatoes, cut into 1/2-inch slices

1 white onion, cut into 1/2-inch slices

1/4 cup and 1 Tbs olive oil

1 lb shrimp, shelled and deveined

1/4 cup fresh parsley, chopped

Layer yellow onions on the bottom of a large pot. Follow with a layer of eggplant and then one of zucchini. Mash the garlic and sprinkle over the zucchini. Continue layering with green peppers, tomatoes, and white onions. Repeat the layering until all vegetables are used. Drizzle 1/4 cup of oil on top and cover.

Bake at 250° F for 6 hours. Remove from the oven. Raise heat to 400° F. Place shrimp on top of the vegetables and drizzle remaining oil over top. Cover and bake for 10 minutes more. Garnish with parsley.

4 servings

🐟

PASTA WITH SHELLFISH AND HERBS

This dish reminds me of the soft, slow nights we spent at seaside restaurants during our honeymoon on Majorca. And for that reason alone, sentimentalist that I am, I love it.

3 Tbs lemon juice
3 Tbs lime juice
1 lb scallops
2 lobsters (about 1-1/4 lbs
     each)
1 cup water
1 cup olive oil

6 scallions, chopped
1 Tbs thyme, minced
1 Tbs basil, minced
1 Tbs oregano, minced
3/4 lb angel-hair pasta
     (nonwheat), cooked

Combine juices in a large bowl, add the scallops, cover and marinate in the refrigerator for 1 hour.

In a large pot, steam the lobsters in 1 cup of water over medium-high heat for 7 minutes. Drain and cool. Remove lobster meat from the shell and cut into scallop-sized pieces.

Add the oil, lobster, scallions, scallops, juices, and herbs to the pasta, mix well, and refrigerate. Allow dish to marinate for an hour.

4 servings

??

CHINESE SQUID SALAD

3/4 cup sesame oil

3 Tbs gingerroot

4 squid fillets, cut into strips, or 10 whole cleaned squid, cut into rings

Juice of 1 lemon

1-1/2 heads of Belgian endive, chopped

1 bunch spinach, stems removed and chopped

1/4 tsp sesame seeds

"Vinaigrette" (see Chapter 8)

2 Tbs vegetable oil

1 tomato, chopped

Combine sesame oil and ginger in a large bowl. Add the squid and mix well. Cover and refrigerate overnight. Then add the lemon juice.

Combine endive, spinach, and sesame seeds in a large mixing bowl. Add 1/8 cup of "vinaigrette" and mix well. Remove squid from marinade and sauté in hot oil quickly, about 1 minute. Place endive and spinach on plates, top with the calamari and tomatoes.

2 servings

&a

SHRIMP KEBABS

Another of those simple, grilled entrées we love so much. I think I could live solely on grilled food. With this recipe, for instance, just paint some sliced zucchini, red bell pepper, and red onion with olive oil, and grill next to the shrimp. Start the veggies first, however, since they take longer to cook. Grill a little polenta next to them, and you've got a complete, delicious dinner. Hotcha!

20 oz large shrimp, shelled and rinsed	1 garlic clove, minced
Juice of 3 lemons	1/8 cup cilantro, chopped
2 Tbs olive oil	Cilantro sprigs
1 small onion, grated	

Place shrimp, lemon juice, and olive oil in a bowl. Marinate for 5 hours. Then add the onion, garlic, and chopped cilantro. Marinate another hour.

Thread shrimp on skewers. Grill or broil until shrimp are done, 2 to 3 minutes. Entwine sprigs of cilantro on skewer and serve.

4 servings

ت

CALAMARI WITH LIME AND GINGER

This is elegant and delicious, and goes nicely with inexpensive chardonnay (which you can serve from a Chalone bottle if there are wine snobs coming).

Maybe you like tentacles. I personally am given pause by them. It's their appearance. They remind me of the villains from fifties science fiction films. I keep thinking they're going to jump on my face and suck my brains out through my nose.

3 Tbs oriental sesame oil
3 Tbs peanut oil
2 lbs squid, cleaned, cut into 1/4-inch pieces (if possible, buy already cleaned and sliced; this is labor intensive, and some stores will do it for you)
2 green onions, chopped
2 Tbs peeled fresh ginger, finely chopped
Juice of 1 lime
1/4 lb softened butter

Heat oils in a large skillet or wok. Add squid and sauté until opaque, about 1 minute. Remove squid to plate and keep warm. Add onion, ginger, and lime juice to pan and boil down rapidly, scraping up any bits from the bottom of the pan. When reduced by half, remove from heat and gradually whisk in butter. Serve squid with sauce poured over.

6 servings

❧

PAELLA

This dish will make you feel like you've been living at the water's edge for nearly a month, in touch with the ebb and flow of the sea, and a simpler, better time.

However, it does cost more to make than the average dish in this book, and you may want to save it for a special feast. Our friend Leslie, who makes a world-famous gumbo, suggests some cayenne pepper. So if you're a hot mama like her, be our guest.

1 medium lobster	1/2 tsp saffron
1/2 cup olive oil	16 oz Chicken broth
2 garlic cloves, minced	15 shrimp, cooked and
1 frying chicken (2–3 lbs),	shelled
cut into small pieces	15 mussels or clams,
3 green peppers, sliced	well scrubbed
4 medium onions	2 cups green peas or
6 medium tomatoes, peeled	sliced green beans
and cut into wedges	1 package (9 oz) ar-
3 cups uncooked rice	tichoke hearts

Cook lobster until red. Remove meat. In a large skillet heat the olive oil and garlic. Sauté the lobster meat over medium heat for 2 or 3 minutes. Remove and reserve. Cook chicken until brown on all sides. Return lobster meat to skillet and add the green peppers, onions, and tomatoes. Cook for about 5 minutes, stirring constantly.

Add the rice and saffron and cook for another 5 minutes. Add chicken broth to cover, plus 1 inch. Cook, covered, over medium heat for 10 minutes, stirring occasionally. Add the shrimp, mussels, peas or beans, and artichokes. Cover and cook for 10 minutes more or until the rice is tender, stirring frequently. If necessary, add more chicken broth, a little at a time. Cook until the paella is dry and all the liquid absorbed. Serve hot.

8–10 servings

&·

MONKFISH AND AVOCADO

Another tasty yet simple dish. Monkfish tastes a bit like lobster, so if you're feeling daring and fancy-free, try lobster pieces instead of the fish.

1 can (12 oz) tomato juice
2 Tbs vegetable oil
1 Tbs lime juice
1/4 tsp ground ginger
1 lb monkfish or sword-
fish, cut into 1-1/2-inch
pieces

1 avocado, peeled and
cut into 1-1/2-inch
pieces
1 Tbs cornstarch
1 Tbs parsley, chopped

Mix together tomato juice, oil, lime juice, and ginger in a large bowl. Place fish in the marinade and refrigerate 1 hour, covered.

Remove fish from marinade, reserving marinade, and thread fish on skewer, alternating with avocado pieces.

Combine reserved marinade, cornstarch, and parsley in 1-quart saucepan. Stir until blended. Cook over medium heat until slightly thickened, stirring constantly.

Broil fish until done or about 10 minutes, basting and turning frequently. Serve with sauce.

4 servings

Vegetarian Dishes

❧

VEGETABLE STIR-FRY

1/4 cup olive oil
3 garlic cloves, crushed
2 yellow bell peppers,
  cored and cut into
  1-inch pieces
2 red bell peppers, cored
  and cut into 1-inch
  pieces

1 lb tomatoes, peeled,
  seeded, and chopped
1 10-oz package frozen
  peas, thawed and
  drained
1 large onion, chopped
1/4 cup butter

Heat the oil in a wok or large skillet. Add garlic and stir until just brown. Add peppers and stir-fry for 2 minutes. Add tomatoes, peas, onions, and butter and stir until heated through.

Transfer to a platter using a slotted spoon. Boil the remaining liquid until thick, about 5 minutes, then pour over vegetables. Serve on rice.

6 servings

🍂

EGGPLANT AND CHICK-PEA CASSEROLE

My first awareness of chick-peas came at the notorious New York nightspot of the sixties and seventies, Max's Kansas City. There was a dish of them on every table, and you could watch the celebrities and drug addicts snacking on them. Rest assured, though—this recipe is very wholesome, another of those soulful vegetarian meals that you think will heal you all by themselves. Try it.

1/4 cup plus 2 Tbs vegetable oil
1-1/2 tsp cumin seeds
1/2 tsp fennel seeds
2 medium onions, sliced
12 large garlic cloves, thickly sliced
2 tsp dried mustard
1 tsp curry powder

1 small eggplant, unpeeled, cut into 1/2-inch-thick by 2-inch-long pieces
5 fresh plum tomatoes, quartered lengthwise
1 can (19 oz) chick-peas, rinsed and drained
2 Tbs fresh cilantro, chopped

In a large skillet, heat oil over high heat. Add cumin seeds and cook until dark brown, about 15 seconds. Add fennel seeds and cook for 5 seconds more. Then add the onion and garlic and reduce heat to medium-high. Cook, stirring often, until the onion and garlic are tender, about 5–10 minutes.

Stir in the mustard, curry, and eggplant. Add more oil if necessary. Reduce heat to moderate and cook, stirring gently, until eggplant is limp, about 5 minutes. Add the tomatoes and cook, stirring constantly, until soft, about 5 minutes. Gently stir in the chick-peas, cover, and simmer over low heat until liquid is thickened, about 5 minutes.

Sprinkle cilantro on top and serve.

6 servings

❧

EGGPLANT CURRY

You say you're too tired to deal with cooking a recipe tonight? Try this: Cut that eggplant you bought in 1/2-inch slices. Paint with a good olive oil. Grill or broil until golden brown. Eat. Roll eyes in pleasure. Watch TV.

1 large eggplant	1/2 tsp turmeric
1 onion, thinly sliced	1 garlic clove, sliced
1 Tbs olive oil	1 large tomato, chopped
1 tsp cumin	3 Tbs cilantro, chopped

Preheat oven to 400° F. Poke the eggplant with a fork, then bake for 1 hour at 400° F. Remove from the oven, slice open, and let liquid drain for 30 minutes. Then cut into 1-inch cubes.

Meanwhile, sauté the onion in olive oil over medium-high heat until golden brown. Add cumin, turmeric, and garlic. Sauté an additional minute, then add tomato and cook on high until most of the liquid is gone. Add eggplant and cilantro. Heat through.

4 servings

❧

THIRTY-MINUTE RATATOUILLE

We find with most ratatouille recipes that the more you cook them, the better they taste. It has something to do with the melding of all the subtle vegetable flavors. But if you don't have the time or inclination for lengthy cooking, try this recipe—the short version. It's really good. Still, if you're hankering for that extra flavor and texture, all you have to do is let this simmer a while longer. This also is one of those dishes that taste better the next day.

2 red peppers, cored and cut into strips	1 small eggplant, halved lengthwise and sliced
2 green peppers, cored and cut into strips	1 onion, sliced
1/4 cup olive oil	Coriander (to taste)
2 zucchini, sliced	

Sauté the peppers in a wok or large skillet in 1 tablespoon of olive oil until tender, about 3–4 minutes, then remove. Add another tablespoon of olive oil and stir-fry zucchini until browned, about 3–4 minutes, then remove. Add another tablespoon of olive oil and stir-fry eggplant until browned, about 3–4 minutes, then remove.

Heat remaining tablespoon of olive oil and stir-fry onion 3 minutes until browned. Add all the other vegetables and the coriander and heat through.

6 servings

ᡧ

VEGETABLE SKILLET

For you folks who think vegetarian food is something that leaves you hungry again a half hour later, try this—it sticks to your ribs. What you are essentially doing with the eggs is poaching them in the pan juices. It may take a little longer to do this than you expect, so be patient. Then serve...and break the yolks so they run all over the food. Seriously delicious.

2 tsp olive oil
1 onion, minced
1 garlic clove, minced
1 eggplant, peeled and
    chopped into cubes

1 leek, carefully washed
    and cut into thin
    slices
2 tomatoes, peeled and
    diced
4 eggs
    chopped parsley

Heat the olive oil in a large skillet. Add the onion and garlic. Sauté until onion is tender. Add the eggplant, leek, and tomatoes. Stir well. Reduce heat, cover, and simmer for 20 minutes.

Uncover. Using bottom of large spoon, make 4 "nests" in the cooking vegetables. Break eggs into nests. Simmer until eggs are poached to desired doneness, sprinkle with parsley, and serve.

4 servings

❧

CABBAGE AND TOMATO CURRY

This is one of our favorite recipes in the whole book. The cabbage has a wonderful crunchy texture, and the spices are delicious. I could eat this every night.

When you add the cabbage, you may think you've chopped up too much—it seems to make a small mountain in the pan. Don't worry, it cooks down fast.

1 Tbs oil	1 Tbs curry powder
1-1/2 tsp black mustard seeds (use plain mustard seeds if you can't find these)	3/4 cabbage, chopped
	1 onion, chopped
	3 tomatoes, coarsely chopped
1/4 tsp fennel seeds	1 Tbs cilantro, minced

Heat the oil in a large skillet over high heat. Add the mustard seeds and sauté until hot. Then add the fennel seeds, browning slightly. (These operations don't take long.) Add the curry powder, cabbage, and onion. Sauté for 5 minutes. Finally add the tomatoes and cilantro, stirring occasionally, until sauce is thickened. Serve as a side dish, or over rice as a vegetarian dinner.

4 servings

~ 7 ~

Dinner

In most households, including ours, dinner is the one meal of the day when there's a little more time to make things nice, and a little more time to sit down and enjoy it. So don't just eat more rice cakes with nut butter—dine.

The idea is to put a protein, a vegetable, and a grain on your plate, with luck all at the right temperature and degree of doneness. Simple, but complete and perfect.

Vegetables

The most simple, direct, delicious, and wonderful way to eat vegetables is steamed and tossed with butter and herbs.

How long this takes depends on the vegetable. Snap peas cook in three minutes, artichokes can take as long as forty-five. Most take ten to fifteen minutes. In general, your vegetable is at the right degree of doneness when the tines of a fork are *just* beginning to slip in easily.

Herbs wonderfully enhance vegetables. Chop them and allow them to sit in hot butter awhile—some of their flavor goes into the butter and makes eating vegetables a truly sensual experience. Here are some good combinations:

Vegetable	*Accompaniment*
Artichoke	Butter, garlic butter, hollandaise
Asparagus	Butter, lemon juice, hollandaise
Beets	Butter, dill, chives, thyme, lemon juice, orange peel

Broccoli	Butter, dill, rosemary, lemon juice, chopped sun-dried tomatoes
Brussels Sprouts	Butter, basil, chives, dill weed, minced parsley, rosemary, thyme, chopped pecans
Carrots	Butter, basil, chives, dill weed, ginger, mint, nutmeg, minced parsley, lemon juice
Cauliflower	Butter, chives, dill weed, nutmeg, minced parsley, lemon juice, hollandaise
Corn	Butter, butter with curry powder, lime juice
Cucumber	Butter, chervil, chives, dill weed, minced parsley
Eggplant	Garlic butter, basil, oregano, marjoram, minced parsley
Green Beans	Butter, dill weed, thyme, chives
Okra	Butter, lemon juice, chopped chives, minced parsley
Peas	Butter, nutmeg, tarragon, chives, thyme
Spinach	Butter, nutmeg, grated lemon peel
Squash (summer)	Butter, basil, oregano, dill weed
Squash (winter)	Butter, nutmeg, cinnamon

Sweet Potatoes	Butter, lemon peel and juice, chopped pecans, cinnamon, nutmeg
Swiss Chard	Butter, basil, nutmeg, oregano
Turnips	Butter, basil, dill, caraway seeds

Here are some other wonderful vegetable dishes that are on target for your diet:

ᴥ

SPAGHETTI SQUASH WITH BUTTER SAUCE

Mmm—nicely goopy. Puts that little sensual hit in your evening. Since spag-squash, as I have come to call it, is relatively bland, you can think of it as a canvas to make individual and beautiful art upon. Try a dash of nutmeg, or chopped scallions, or toasted pine nuts, or chopped sun-dried tomatoes...

1 spaghetti squash	1 tsp chopped fresh
2 Tbs butter or margarine	oregano (dry is also
1 garlic clove, pressed	serviceable)

Cut spaghetti squash in half lengthwise, clean out the innards, and spread liberally with butter or margarine. Put plastic wrap over both halves, put in microwave, and cook at 5-minute intervals, turning each time, until squash is relatively soft, about 10–12 minutes.

While the squash is cooking, melt butter in a small skillet. Add garlic and oregano and cook over low heat for 10 minutes.

When squash is finished, run fork through squash to make "spaghetti." Toss with butter mixture and serve.

4 servings

❧

CINNAMON PARSNIPS

So simple, so good. And you have the fun of watching your guests' stunned expressions when they ask you what vegetable that is, and you tell them. "Wow," they'll think, "she knows about parsnips."

1/2 lb parsnips, peeled, trimmed, and shredded	2 Tbs butter, softened 1/2 tsp cinnamon

Steam the parsnips in a vegetable steamer, covered, for 3 minutes or until just tender.

In a heated bowl toss parsnips with butter and cinnamon.

2 servings

🙾

ZUCCHINI AND PEPPER MIX

1 Tbs unsalted butter   1/2 lb zucchini, sliced
1 red bell pepper, cut into
    1/2-inch pieces

In a large skillet, add butter and cook the bell pepper,
covered, over medium-low heat for 5 minutes, stirring
occasionally. Add zucchini and cook, stirring occasionally, for
6 minutes or until zucchini is tender.

2 servings

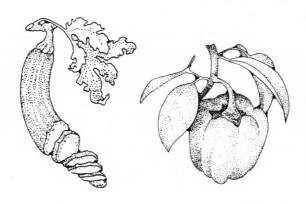

❧

FENNEL AND LEEKS

1 large fennel bulb, chopped into 1/4-inch pieces

12 garlic cloves, peeled

1 Tbs extra-virgin olive oil

4 medium leeks (about 1 lb), chopped into 1/4-inch pieces

Preheat oven to 450° F. Place a sheet of heavy-duty aluminum foil about 2 feet by 1 foot on a work surface. Arrange fennel and half the garlic cloves on one half of foil. Drizzle with 1/2 tablespoon of olive oil. Fold empty half of the foil over fennel and crimp the edges to form a tight seal. Place the package on a baking sheet.

Do the same with the leeks, placing them and the 6 remaining garlic cloves on a large sheet of aluminum foil. Drizzle with remaining olive oil. Fold the foil over, seal, and place package on the same baking sheet with fennel.

Bake vegetables for 10 minutes. Then flip the packages over and bake for 15 more minutes. Remove from the oven and let stand without opening for 5 minutes. Remove vegetables from foil and mix together in a medium bowl. Serve.

This can be served warm or put in the refrigerator and served at a later time, chilled.

4 servings

❧

BRAISED FENNEL

I discovered fennel one day when Mary and I were playing baseball in a vacant lot with our hip friends Eva and Rex. Someone whacked the ball into an anonymous patch of greenery—and this fabulous licorice scent suddenly ravished us. It turned out fennel just grows wild, and we were able to dig up a few bulbs and braise them. It was love at first smell—and taste.

The more butter you whisk in at the end, the more sumptuous things become. This is an unabashedly sensual dish. You could be excommunicated for eating this.

6 medium fennel bulbs with fronds	1/4 cup butter or olive oil
1 smallish onion, sliced	1 cup chicken broth
1 garlic clove, minced	1 sprig thyme
1 small carrot, grated	Up to 3 Tbs of butter
Few celery leaves, chopped	

Remove fronds. Quarter bulbs. Sauté onion, garlic, carrot, and celery leaves nice and easily in 1/4 cup butter.

Sauté fennel quarters on all sides. Add broth and thyme sprig. Bring to boil, reduce heat, cover, and simmer until fennel is tender, about 25 minutes. Test with fork for doneness.

Remove fennel to warmed serving dish; tent with foil. Boil down pan liquids by 2/3 or more until somewhat thick. Discard thyme sprig. Whisk in remaining butter to taste and pour over fennel in the serving dish.

6 servings

❧

PARSNIP AND BEET FRY

This recipe strike anyone as a little, well, off the beaten path? Possibly it's been some time since you hazarded a parsnip. Well, I guarantee you a major taste treat here. Really, there were four grown people at our table one night fighting for the last helping. And these were people who had earlier exclaimed "Parsnip and Beet Fry? Eyew!" I guess you could say this recipe falls into the mind-blower category.

1 medium beet, unpeeled	3 Tbs butter
1 medium parsnip, peeled and grated	1 Tbs shallot, minced
1/4 tsp dried thyme, crumbled	Fresh thyme sprigs

Preheat oven to 350° F. Place the beet in a small baking pan and bake until tender, about 1 hour. Grate and toss with parsnip and crumbled thyme.

Melt 1 tablespoon butter in a heavy skillet over medium heat. Add shallot and stir for 30 seconds. Then add the beet and parsnip mixture and cook for 3 minutes.

Add the remaining 2 tablespoons butter and cook over low heat, stirring occasionally, for 10 minutes. Sprinkle with thyme sprigs and serve.

2 servings

❧

BRAISED ROOT VEGETABLES

This is one of my favorite vegetable recipes. It's a standby on Thanksgiving, and all through the winter months. It's so delicious my guests freak out. "This is great,*" they cry out, and demand the recipe. Whether they get it or not depends on what wine they brought. But you get it for free!*

1/4 cup butter
4 garlic cloves, peeled
1 onion, sliced
1/2 lb carrots, peeled and
    cut into diagonal pieces

1 lb sweet potatoes,
    peeled and thickly
    sliced
1/2 lb parsnips, peeled
    and cut into diagonal
    pieces
2 Tbs chopped parsley

Melt half the butter in a large skillet. Add garlic and onion, and cook until tender. Then add carrots, potatoes, parsnips, and water to cover. Bring to a boil. Simmer covered until vegetables are just tender but not mushy, about 20 minutes.

Uncover and bring to a rapid boil. When liquid has evaporated, add remaining butter in pieces, stirring so vegetables are fully coated, and sprinkle with parsley.

6 servings

❧

SAUTÉED EGGPLANT

Elegant, straightforward, fine. How to put nice vegetables on your plate without straining.

2 Tbs olive oil	1 garlic clove, minced
1 Japanese eggplant, thinly sliced	1 tomato, chopped

Add the olive oil to a large skillet and sauté eggplant until browned on both sides. Drain on paper towels.

In the same pan, sauté garlic, then add the tomato and cook until soft. Add the eggplant and reheat.

2 servings

❧

BRAISED KALE

We love greens. No, not that German political group—though they seem very nice—but all those things like collards, kale, beet greens, chard, and so forth. Very, very healthy. And with a kind of soulful quality that's very appealing. Try this one.

1 small onion, finely chopped	1 lb kale, stems removed, chopped
1 Tbs butter	1 Tbs lemon juice

In a large skillet, sauté the onion in butter until tender, about 5 minutes.

Meanwhile, rinse the kale in cold water, add to the skillet, and simmer covered 15–20 minutes, stirring occasionally.

Sprinkle with lemon juice.

4 servings

❧

BRUSSELS SPROUTS AND CARROTS

I know, brussels sprouts. You hate 'em, right? You're making a face like my kid makes when I offer him broccoli. But I swear, this is delicious. The lemon flavor works magic. Trust me.

1 lb brussels sprouts, trimmed and cut in half	1/3 cup butter
	1 tsp caraway seeds
1 lb carrots, peeled and cut in half lengthwise and then crosswise	1 garlic clove, minced
	Grated peel of lemon
	2 Tbs lemon juice

In a large skillet, cook brussels sprouts and carrots in 1 inch of boiling water until tender, about 10–15 minutes. Drain well and set vegetables aside.

In the same pan, melt the butter and add the caraway seeds, garlic, lemon peel, and lemon juice. Add the cooked vegetables and heat.

6 servings

🕭

BRUSSELS SPROUTS WITH PECAN BUTTER

Aw, jeez, here we come with our brussels sprouts again. Listen, people, you have to trust us on this. Gussied up properly, the little green guys are delicious. Even my own mother wouldn't trust me! Of course, she'd been forced to eat them (probably totally overcooked) at boarding school as a girl and was traumatized, suffering Forced Brussels Sprouts Syndrome. What's your excuse? Now, cook some of this up and check it out, okay?

3/4 cup pecans, minced   2 lbs brussels sprouts
4 Tbs butter

Cook pecans over low heat in butter until lightly browned, about 15 minutes.

Wash brussels sprouts. Trim off outside leaves. Steam until tender.

In a large frying pan, add the pecan butter and brussels sprouts and heat through, stirring occasionally.

4–6 servings

❧

ZUCCHINI GREEK STYLE

3 Tbs olive oil
1 garlic clove, minced
1 small onion
1 lb zucchini, in 1/4-inch
 slices

2 tomatoes, skinned and
 chopped
1/2 tsp oregano
1 Tbs chopped parsley

Heat the oil in a large skillet. Sauté garlic and onion until tender.

Add zucchini, simmer covered until almost tender, about 5 minutes. Stir in tomatoes, oregano, and parsley. Simmer 2 more minutes.

4 servings

Grains and Beans

We'll assume you know the rudiments of cooking grains and beans or have cookbooks that can teach you.

Rice made with chicken broth is more sumptuous than that made with water.

Check out the many good boxed rice and grain dishes available at health food stores. Many of them are delicious and dietetically correct. See examples in Chapter 3—Shopping.

Also, don't forget lentils. They are healthy, cheap, and easily prepared...and can be made in countless delicious ways.

Here are some recipes:

❧

WILD RICE

Crunchy. That's what a lot of rice dishes should be and aren't. This never-fail-to-get-a-compliment wild rice recipe is a super-delicious crowd-pleaser.

1/4 lb wild rice	1/2 stalk celery, minced
21/2 cups water	2 Tbs butter
1/4 cup pine nuts	1/2 cup chicken broth
1/2 onion, minced	

Cook rice in water over low heat for 50 minutes or until tender and then drain.

In a saucepan sauté pine nuts, onion, and celery in butter over medium heat for 10 minutes. Add rice and chicken broth and cook, stirring until chicken broth is absorbed, about 5–10 minutes.

2–4 servings

❧

SPICY WILD RICE

If you would like this to actually be spicy, as its name suggests, better add some salt and pepper.

2 Tbs butter
1 carrot, diced
1 celery stalk, diced
1 leek, carefully washed
   and diced

2 cups wild rice
4 cups chicken broth
   and additional broth
   as needed

Heat butter over medium-low heat. Add carrot, celery, and leek. Cook, stirring occasionally, for about 1 minute. Stir in rice and add the chicken broth, cover, and cook slowly until rice is done, about 1 hour and 15 minutes. Add extra chicken broth as needed.

8 servings

ᴥ

LENTIL PILAF

Don't rice and lentils and stuff taste healthy? *And, in fact, they are! But what's great is they're* deliciously *healthy.*

1 bunch green onions,
  chopped
2 garlic cloves, minced
1 cup lentils, rinsed
1/2 cup brown rice, rinsed
1/4 cup wild rice, rinsed

1/4 cup butter
2 Tbs slivered almonds
1/2 tsp dried thyme
  leaves, crushed
2-1/2 cups chicken broth

In a large skillet, sauté the onions, garlic, lentils, and both rices in butter until the onion is tender, about 4 minutes. Add the almonds, thyme, and chicken broth and bring to a boil. Reduce heat and simmer, covered, for about 30 minutes or until liquid is absorbed.

6 servings

❧

RED BEANS AND RICE JOHNNY OTIS

This is labor-intensive. It is, however, nutritionally complete, so if you make it, you won't have to cook anything else that night. And it's much easier with canned kidney beans; you won't need to soak them overnight. Buy two 16-ounce cans of kidney beans—that's roughly equivalent to 1 pound of dried beans.

We got into red beans and rice thanks to R&B progenitor Johnny Otis, who throws an annual "Red Beans and Rice Cookoff" here in California, featuring great soul and blues artists. So we're naming our recipe after him. Thanks, Johnny.

Beans:

1 lb dried red kidney beans	4 garlic cloves, minced
2 cups onion, chopped	4 cups chicken broth
1/4 cup olive oil	2 bay leaves

Rice:

2 Tbs olive oil	2 cups long-grain rice,
1/2 cup onion, chopped	freshly cooked

Beans: Place beans in a bowl, cover with water, and let soak for 24 hours. Drain and set aside.

In a large saucepan sauté onion in olive oil over low heat until it's golden brown, about 15 minutes. Add garlic and sauté another 3 minutes. Add beans and broth, bring to a boil, then reduce heat, cover, and simmer for 2 hours. Then add bay leaves. Cover and continue simmering until beans are tender, about 1 more hour. Transfer to a bowl and keep warm.

Rice: Heat oil in a large skillet over medium-low heat. Add the onion and sauté until tender, about 10 minutes. Add the rice and heat through.

Serve rice and beans side by side or place the rice in bowls and top with beans.

6 servings

❧

MARY'S CASSOULET

Labor-intensive, but worth it. Save effort by using canned white beans—two 16-ouncers ought to do it. Great Northern's good.

This gets five yums on the yum scale. It's a real cassoulet, with hearty flavors that are a perfect match with cool autumn evenings, a fire in the fireplace, and a nice Côtes du Rhone.

1 lb dry white beans	5 chicken thighs
1 carrot, sliced	2 Tbs oil
1/4 tsp dried thyme	1/2 cup onion, chopped
1 onion, studded with 6 cloves	2 garlic cloves, minced
1/4 lb veal	3 Tbs butter

Soak beans overnight in water, making sure the water covers the beans. The next day add the carrot, thyme, and whole onion studded with cloves to the pot. Stir. Bring the mixture to a boil, reduce heat, and simmer, covered, for 1-1/2 hours. Add more water if needed.

Place the veal in a small pan, cover with boiling water, and cook for 10 minutes. Remove from the pan, dice, and add to the beans.

In a large frying pan, add the chicken and sauté until well browned. Remove the chicken and set aside. Add the 1/2 cup onion and garlic to the pan and cook in remaining drippings until tender.

Add the onion and garlic mixture to the beans. When finished, layer beans and chicken into a 3-quart casserole. Cover and bake at 250° F for 3 hours, adding water as needed if cassoulet becomes too dry.

4 servings

Pasta

The bad news about pasta is that it's generally made from wheat and wheat is allowed only if you're not allergic to it. The good news is there are now pastas available made from a mixture of quinoa, a South American grain that's on your approved list, and corn flour, which is also no problem. The brand we found is Ancient Harvest, and it comes in several shapes. Look for quinoa, amaranth, and corn pasta as well as Japanese buckwheat noodles at your local health food store. Remember, vegetable noodles are mainly wheat and should be introduced only when you've started the Phase Two diet.

🕮

PASTA WITH TOMATO AND GARLIC

The length of time you will need to simmer the tomatoes depends on their degree of ripeness. Very ripe tomatoes quickly liquify when heated; less ripe ones hold their shape much longer. Since our taste is to have some tomato chunks with our pasta, we barely heat the tomatoes through before tossing with the pasta.

1 lb pasta	12 plum tomatoes,
6 garlic cloves, minced	chopped
1/4 cup olive oil	2/3 cup parsley, chopped

Cook pasta according to package directions. Drain.

Meanwhile, in a medium skillet, sauté the garlic in the oil over medium heat until soft, about 3 minutes. Add the tomatoes and parsley, lower heat, and simmer a short time. Toss pasta with sauce and serve.

4 servings

&✿

PASTA AND TUNA

Simple, easy, good. They sell olive-oil-packed tuna in Italian delis. If you have the kind packed in water, add a bit of good-tasting olive oil that you keep in your cabinet for moments like this.

3 Tbs olive oil
1 large onion, chopped
3 scallions, minced
2 6-1/2-oz cans tuna fish
    packed in olive oil
3 cups tomato sauce

1/4 cup green pepper,
    chopped
3 Tbs fresh parsley,
    chopped
1 lb pasta

In a large pot, heat oil, then add onion and scallions and sauté until golden. Stir in tuna, with its own oil, breaking into small pieces. (If tuna is packed in water, discard water and add another tablespoon of olive oil.)

Cook over medium heat for 2 minutes. Cool for a moment, then add the tomato sauce, pepper, and 1 tablespoon of parsley. Simmer for 5 minutes, then remove from heat and let stand while cooking the pasta.

Cook the pasta in 6 quarts of boiling water until *al dente*. See package directions for cooking time, or test from time to time. Drain thoroughly in a colander. Put pasta on plates, top with sauce. Sprinkle with remaining parsley.

4 servings

❧

PASTA WITH RED AND GREEN PEPPERS

I also cook this with red and yellow peppers instead of the green ones, which makes for a sweeter, more succulent meal. If you don't feel like roasting the peppers—don't. The dish is just fine with the peppers sautéed.

1/2 lb pasta
2 Tbs butter
2 Tbs olive oil
8 sun-dried tomatoes, packed in oil, chopped
1/4 cup fresh basil

1/4 cup chopped fresh parsley
4 garlic cloves, minced
2 sweet red peppers, cut in strips
2 green peppers, cut in strips

Cook the pasta in boiling water until *al dente*, following package directions. Drain.

Meanwhile, in a saucepan heat butter and olive oil. Add the tomatoes, basil, parsley, garlic, and peppers. Sauté until heated through.

Add the pepper and tomato mixture to the pasta and mix well.

4 servings

&❧

LENTILS AND PASTA

This defines "earthy." I mean that as a compliment.

1 cup dried lentils	3 garlic cloves, minced
4 cups water	2 tsp ground cilantro
2 Tbs olive oil	1/2 lb pasta
1 cup onions, finely chopped	3 Tbs butter

Boil the lentils and water in a medium saucepan. Reduce heat and simmer, uncovered, until lentils are tender, about 1 hour. Add more water as needed. Drain.

Meanwhile, heat the olive oil in a large skillet. Add the onions, garlic, and cilantro, sauté until the onion is tender, about 10 minutes.

Cook the pasta in boiling water until *al dente*, following package directions. Drain.

Add the pasta, lentils, and butter to a large skillet. Cook over low heat, stirring occasionally, until butter is melted. Add the onion mixture, heat thoroughly, and serve.

6 servings

🐚

PASTA WITH CRAB SAUCE

4 oz spaghetti
1 Tbs butter
1/2 cup green onions,
    chopped
1 garlic clove, minced
2 medium tomatoes,
    peeled, seeded, and
    chopped

1/4 cup chicken broth
1/2 lb cooked crabmeat,
    shredded
1 Tbs lemon juice
1/2 tsp celery salt
1/4 cup fresh parsley,
    chopped

Cook the pasta in boiling water until *al ∂ente*, following package directions. Drain.

Melt the butter in a large skillet, sauté onions and garlic until tender, about 3 minutes. Add the tomatoes and chicken broth, increase the heat, and bring to a boil, stirring constantly. Reduce the heat and simmer for 2 minutes. Add the crab, lemon juice, and celery salt. Cook until heated through, about 2 minutes. Stir in the chopped parsley.

Put the pasta on a serving dish. Top with the crab mixture.

2 servings

🐌

PASTA WITH FENNEL

1/2 lb linguine or angel hair pasta	2 tsp water
2 tsp olive oil	2 cups Fennel and Leeks (Chapter 7)

Cook the pasta to taste according to package directions. Drain.

Put the olive oil and 2 teaspoons of water in a medium skillet over medium heat. Stir in vegetables, cover, and cook until heated through.

Add the pasta and mix well.

2 servings

❧

PASTA WITH SHRIMP

This is fine cold at a picnic. People will think you bought it at Dean & Deluca or somewhere.

Remember I was telling you about how salt makes a lot of these recipes taste better? Well, this is definitely one of them.

1 lb pasta
1 lb medium shrimp,
    shelled and deveined
1/4 cup olive oil plus 2 Tbs
2 shallots, chopped
8 sun-dried tomatoes
    packed in oil, cut into
    strips

1 tsp dried oregano
2 small bunches arugula,
    stems removed,
    chopped
1-1/2 tsp lemon juice

Cook the pasta in boiling water until *al dente*, according to package directions. Drain.

Meanwhile, sauté the shrimp in 2 tablespoons of olive oil in a medium skillet until pink, about 2 minutes.

Add the shallots, sun-dried tomatoes, and oregano. Cook, stirring occasionally, until shallots are soft, about 2 minutes. Scrape the mixture into a large bowl.

Add the arugula, 1/4 cup olive oil, and lemon juice. Stir well.

Add the pasta and mix well.

4 servings

🕊

CILANTRO CHICKEN WITH PASTA

Here's an easy recipe for 8. Let your spouse clean up.

To keep the chicken skin from sticking to the pan, dry chicken before sautéing and keep heat moderate. If skin does stick, the chicken will still taste fine, but it may look as if somebody already ate it.

8 chicken legs	Juice of 2 lemons
8 chicken thighs	3/4 cup fresh cilantro,
1/2 cup olive oil	chopped
4 tsp cumin seeds	4 cups chicken broth
1 tsp saffron threads	2 cups small dried pasta

Place chicken legs and thighs in a glass baking dish. In a bowl, combine the oil, cumin seeds, saffron, lemon juice, and 1/2 cup of the cilantro. Pour over the chicken and turn to coat. Cover and marinate at room temperature for 1 hour or up to 4 hours in the refrigerator.

Heat 2 large, deep, heavy skillets over moderate heat. Give each skillet 1/4 cup of oil and cook chicken, turning frequently until browned, about 15 minutes. Remove chicken to warmed plate and set aside.

Pour all the fat from the pans. Add 2 cups of broth to each pan and bring to a boil over high heat, scraping to dislodge any bits from the bottom. Pour all the broth into one pan, add the pasta, and cook for 4 minutes, stirring frequently.

Return the chicken to the pasta pan. Reduce heat, cover tightly, and simmer until the pasta and chicken are cooked thoroughly, about 20 minutes. Transfer chicken to plates and sprinkle remaining cilantro on top. Serve pasta alongside.

8 servings

Seafood

With fish, you can do a lot of substituting. Though a given recipe may call for swordfish, salmon would be fine, or shark, or halibut steaks. Buy what's on special and feel free to experiment.
See additional seafood recipes in Chapter 6—Lunch.

❧

MARINATED SWORDFISH WITH CILANTRO BUTTER

Simple, elegant, easy, delicious. These are words more recipes would like to have said about them.

4 6-oz swordfish (or tuna
    or shark) steaks
Juice of 2 limes
1/2 cup butter

1 garlic clove, minced
3/4 cup fresh cilantro,
    chopped
Lime wedges

Put the fish in a glass baking dish. Pour the lime juice over. Marinate in the refrigerator for at least a half hour.
Melt the butter in a small saucepan. Add the garlic and cook for 30 seconds. Mix in the cilantro and cook until heated through, about 1 minute.
On a medium-hot grill, cook the fish about 8–10 minutes, depending on thickness or desired doneness, basting often with the cilantro butter.
Serve fish with lime wedges.

4 servings

🙞

SWORDFISH WITH MINT AND LEMON BUTTER

6 Tbs unsalted butter,
  room temperature
4 tsp fresh mint, minced
1 tsp lemon peel, grated

4 6-oz swordfish steaks
1/4 cup extra-virgin
  olive oil
Fresh mint leaves

Start grill or preheat broiller. Mix the first 3 ingredients in a small bowl. Shape the butter into a log, cover with wax paper, and refrigerate.

Put the fish in a shallow baking dish and drizzle with oil. Grill or broil fish until pink inside, about 4 minutes a side. Transfer the fish to plates, then top with a thick slice of mint and lemon butter. Garnish with mint leaves.

4 servings

NOTE: Butter can be made 1 day in advance and be kept up to a month in the freezer.

🐌

SWORDFISH IN TOMATO AND FENNEL SAUCE

That licoricy fennel taste pervades this, thanks to the fennel seeds. You might want to give them a couple of bashes in a mortar and pestle before throwing them in, to release even more flavor.

2 Tbs olive oil	1/2 tsp fennel seeds
1 small fennel bulb, trimmed, quartered, and sliced crosswise (you can substitute 2 celery stalks, sliced 1/4-inch-thick), reserving fennel tops	1 orange peel strip, diced
	3 lemon peel strips, diced
	1 16-oz can Italian plum tomatoes, undrained
1/2 cup onion, chopped	4 swordfish steaks
1 garlic clove, minced	4 thin lemon slices

Heat oil in a stovetop-to-oven baking dish over medium-low heat. Add fennel and onion and sauté until tender, about 10 minutes. Stir in garlic and sauté 1 minute. Add fennel seeds, orange and lemon peel, and tomatoes with liquid. Bring to boil over low heat, stirring constantly, breaking up tomatoes with spoon. Simmer sauce until reduced slightly, about 10 minutes.

Preheat broiler. Arrange fish on top of the tomato mixture. Broil 2 inches from heat until fish is opaque, about 5 minutes.

Serve fish on heated plates. Spoon on sauce. Garnish with lemon slices and reserved fennel tops.

4 servings

❧

SWORDFISH AND SALSA

This is great grilled, too. And really easy—your guests think they're getting something you slaved over, but it won't take you a half hour.

4 swordfish steaks	Simple Salsa (see
4 Tbs unsalted butter,	Chapter 8)
melted	

Preheat broiler and arrange fish on a broiling rack. Brush each steak with 1/2 tablespoon of melted butter. Broil fish 4 inches from heat for about 4 minutes. Turn steaks over and brush each with 1/2 tablespoon of butter. Broil 4 minutes longer, until fish is opaque. Transfer to a warm plate and top with salsa.

4 servings

🐚

GRILLED SHARK WITH TOMATOES AND HERBS

At one time, I'd never heard of eating shark. I don't know, I guess I thought it was too fierce to eat, that it would eat you back or something. But I went down in one of those underwater cages and let Great Whites lunge at me until my fear went away, and today feel perfectly comfortable eating shark, anywhere, anytime.

3 tomatoes, peeled, seeded, and chopped	2 Tbs chervil, chopped
1/2 cup extra-virgin olive oil	2 Tbs chives, chopped
	2 Tbs tarragon, chopped
3 Tbs lemon juice	4 shark (or tuna or swordfish) steaks
3 garlic cloves, minced	

In a medium bowl, blend together tomatoes, olive oil, lemon juice, and garlic. Set aside for 2 hours. Then add all the herbs, mixing well.

Grill the fish on a preheated broiler 4 inches from the heat, turning once, until charred on the outside, about 3 to 4 minutes on each side.

When the fish is done transfer it onto a large platter and cut it into thick strips. Top with half of the tomato sauce and put the rest of the sauce in a bowl.

4 servings

🎙

SALMON WITH LIME BUTTER

This is an extremely quick and easy recipe. But to make it even easier on yourself, have the butcher make those paper-thin slices for you. We could be saving you a fingertip here, too.

This defines that now familiar litany: easy, quick, delicious.

1 lb salmon fillets	Juice of 1/2 lime
2 shallots, chopped	Lime peel, grated
4 Tbs butter	

Heat oven to 350° F. Put 4 oven-proof plates in preheated oven to warm, about 3 minutes. Then cut salmon into paper-thin slices.

Sauté shallots in butter until slightly brown. Squeeze in lime juice and sprinkle in peel. Stir. When butter sizzles, coat each plate with 1/2 tablespoon of butter and immediately put fish on hot plates. Pour remaining butter over salmon and serve immediately.

4 servings

&ea;

GRILLED TUNA AND EGGPLANT

1/4 cup olive oil
1 1-lb eggplant, cut into
   1/4-inch-thick slices
1 sweet red pepper

1/2 tsp rosemary,
   crumbled
1 lb tuna steak

Preheat broiler.

Heat 2 tablespoons of olive oil in a large skillet over medium-high heat. Add the eggplant and cook until browned on both sides. Add more oil if necessary. Remove from the heat and set aside.

Broil the red pepper about 10 minutes or until all sides are blistered. Put the pepper in a brown paper bag and let stand 10 minutes. Under cold water, gently rub the pepper to peel off the skin. Remove the seeds and slice the pepper.

If desired, chop the eggplant, then combine the eggplant and red pepper with 2 tablespoons olive oil and rosemary. Let stand for 30 minutes.

Grill or broil tuna about 1–3 minutes per side until medium rare. Place the tuna on a serving plate and cover with the eggplant mixture.

4 servings

❧

SHRIMP CREOLE

Mary, who doesn't like celery, wants me to say that if you don't like celery, you have clearance from us to leave it out. The only thing this will change, besides the fact that you won't taste celery, is that you won't have much crunch *left. So if you like crunch but don't like celery, try some chopped fennel.*

1 Tbs butter

2 cups onion, finely chopped

2 cups celery, minced

1 cup green pepper, minced

1 garlic clove, minced

1 tsp fennel seeds

1/2 cup parsley, minced

1 bay leaf

2 sprigs fresh thyme or 1 tsp dried

6 cups canned chopped tomatoes

2 tsp curry powder

2 lbs raw shrimp, shelled and deveined

Heat butter in a medium saucepan. Add onion, celery, green pepper, garlic, and fennel seeds. Cook, stirring until onion is tender, about 5 minutes.

Add remaining ingredients except for shrimp. Bring to a boil and simmer 15 minutes, stirring occasionally.

Add shrimp and cook until done, 5–10 minutes more.

6 servings

❧

SCALLOPS IN HERB BUTTER

The fresh herbs really make this one sing. Serve it in custard cups as a first course, or with rice and a green salad as a main course. Either way, the tarragon is the key. As James Brown once said, "Ow!"

6 Tbs butter	2 lbs bay scallops
4 shallots, peeled and chopped	2 Tbs parsley, chopped
2 garlic cloves, chopped	1 Tbs chives, chopped
	1 Tbs tarragon, chopped

Melt the butter in a sauté pan, add the shallots and garlic, and sauté until tender, about 2 minutes. Then add the scallops and herbs, and sauté until the scallops are cooked, another minute or two. Serve.

For a first course, you can put a quarter pound of scallops each in custard cups, pour the sautéed shallots and garlic on top, and sprinkle the herbs on top. Then bake at 425° F about 10 minutes and serve in cups.

4 servings as entrée, 8 for first course

🙶

RICE PILAF WITH SHRIMP

3 Tbs olive oil

1 lb medium shrimp,
    shelled and deveined

2 small zucchini, cut into
    thin sticks

1/2 cup onion, minced

1 garlic clove, minced

1-1/4 cups long-grain
    rice

2-1/2 cups hot water

1/2 tsp dried thyme,
    crumbled

1 bay leaf

2 Tbs cilantro, minced

Heat 2 tablespoons of oil in a sauté pan. Add the shrimp and sauté for 2 minutes. Remove shrimp. Add the zucchini and sauté for 2 minutes. Remove zucchini.

Add remaining 1 tablespoon of oil to the pan along with the onion. Sauté over medium heat until tender, but not brown, about 7 minutes. Add garlic and rice and sauté another 3 minutes.

Pour the hot water over the rice and stir. Add the thyme and the bay leaf. Bring to a boil over high heat. Then lower heat, cover, and simmer for 25–30 minutes until liquid is absorbed. Scatter the shrimp and zucchini over the top. Simmer, covered, for an additional 3–5 minutes until rice is tender. Discard the bay leaf.

Top with the cilantro.

4 servings

Birds

Here we are referring not to Charlie Parker, but to those small, wing-flapping, squawking things that taste so good with tarragon. Chicken, cornish hen, and turkey, of course. But increasingly pheasant, quail, and other formerly exotic, hard-to-find avians are becoming available. On with the recipes!

❧

GRILLED MARINATED CHICKEN BREASTS

Perfect grill food. Flavor intensity. A major crowd-pleaser.

3/4 cup lemon juice
3/4 cup vegetable oil
1/4 cup onion, minced

1-1/2 tsp thyme
12 chicken breast halves,
   boned and skinned

In a medium bowl, mix together the lemon juice, oil, onion, and thyme. With a sharp knife, make small cuts in each chicken breast. Pour 1/3 of the marinade into a shallow glass bowl or baking dish. Add half the chicken and cover with 1/3 of the marinade. Layer the remaining chicken on top and add the remaining marinade. Let stand in the refrigerator for 3 hours, turning occasionally. Remove from the refrigerator for an hour to bring to room temperature.

Cook chicken on a grill or under a preheated broiler, 3 minutes or more per side. Do not overcook, as breasts will be dry and chewy. To check for doneness, slice into a breast — it should be slightly pink at the center.

6 servings

❧

MIXED GRILL

I make this all the time, and always love it—it's got legs, literally and figuratively. That's because the chicken and shrimp, following their marination, are imbued with all these delicious flavors. You spouses not on the diet could precook a couple of sausages in a pan of boiling water, then add chunks to the skewers. They bring a nice third flavor to this.

1/2 cup olive oil
2 garlic cloves, minced
1 tsp dried sage
1/2 tsp dried thyme
2 Tbs lemon juice

2 chicken thighs, boned, skinned, and cut into 4 pieces each
8 large shrimp
1 red onion, cut in chunks

Mix the first 5 ingredients in a glass bowl. Add the chicken and shrimp and stir. Let stand for 20 minutes.

Heat the grill or broiler.

Drain chicken and shrimp, reserving marinade. Alternating chicken, shrimp, and onion pieces, thread onto skewers. Cook, turning the skewers and basting with marinade until the meat is cooked, 10–15 minutes.

4 servings

ও

SOUTH OF THE BORDER MILLET AND CHICKEN IN LETTUCE

An off-the-beaten-path sort of dinner, perfect in hot weather.

When I first tried this, I wasn't expecting very much. I had this bad association with millet. I'd seen the movie Seven Samurai, *in which it was eaten by miserable, downtrodden villagers so poor they couldn't afford rice. Kinda created a negative image of the stuff for me. Well, wrong again. Obviously. the villagers' problem was they didn't prepare it with canned chicken broth. Millet's great.*

1 cup millet
Chicken broth
1/4 cup lime juice (about 2
    limes)
2 Tbs olive oil
1 garlic clove, pressed
4 green onions, chopped
1/2 cup chopped red bell
    pepper

2 Tbs minced fresh
    coriander
1 cup cooked chicken or
    turkey, chopped
1 cup tomato, chopped
1 cup coriander
    (cilantro), chopped
1 avocado, peeled and
    sliced
12 large lettuce leaves

Cook the millet according to package directions, using chicken broth instead of water. Drain and fluff the millet with a fork. Allow to cool.

Whisk the lime juice, olive oil, and garlic in a large bowl. Add the millet, onions, bell pepper, and minced cilantro, and toss.

Put the chicken or turkey, chopped tomatoes, chopped cilantro, and sliced avocado on separate serving plates.

Arrange lettuce leaves on a platter. Station these pleasingly around the dinner table.

Give everyone a good helping of the millet mixture. Pass the lettuce leaves, then the other ingredients.

4 servings

❧

ROSEMARY CHICKEN BREASTS
WITH SHALLOT BUTTER

*Another perfect grill food. Serve your guests a young chardonnay,
balanced to acid.*

1 shallot	4 large chicken breasts,
6 Tbs softened butter	bone removed
1/2 Tbs fresh ground	1 Tbs oil
pepper	2 Tbs minced fresh
1 lemon, juiced	rosemary

Mince shallot. Beat into butter with pepper. Season to taste
with lemon juice. Roll into 1-inch log, wrap in plastic, and
refrigerate.

Rub breasts with oil and rosemary. Grill or broil chicken,
turning once, until done — about 10 minutes. Top each breast
with a quarter-inch slice of butter and serve.

4 servings

❧

MICROWAVE CHICKEN

2 Tbs olive oil
1 chicken, disjointed,
    breasts halved
1 onion, minced
1 red pepper, cored,
    seeded, and minced
1 garlic clove, minced
1 cup rice, cooked
1 can (12 oz) chopped
    tomatoes with juice

2 tsp paprika
1/2 tsp fennel seeds
1/2 tsp ground coriander
1-1/2 cups frozen peas
2 Tbs water
2 Tbs cilantro, minced

Heat oil in a large, heavy skillet. Add chicken and brown on all sides, about 5 minutes. Transfer to a platter and set aside.

Sauté onion, pepper, and garlic in drippings for 2 minutes. Transfer to a 5-quart microwave casserole.

Stir rice, tomatoes, paprika, fennel, and ground coriander into the casserole. Arrange chicken on top, largest pieces toward the outside, wings in the center.

Cover and microwave on high for 12 minutes. Turn chicken over, stir rice, and rotate dish 180 degrees. Microwave an additional 12 minutes or until chicken is done and rice is tender. (Remember, every microwave is different; some will require more or less cooking time.) Let stand, covered, a few minutes.

Meanwhile, microwave peas with water in covered 1-pint casserole on high for 5 minutes, stirring at 2 minutes. Cook until tender. Drain well. Stir into chicken and rice mixture. Sprinkle with cilantro and serve.

6 servings

❧

CHICKEN AND CILANTRO

A perfect mid-week, throw-together dinner. Just make some rice to go with it. The cilantro gives it a nice flavor intensity.

2-1/2 Tbs vegetable oil
2 small green peppers,
　　sliced into rings
1-1/2 lbs skinless, boneless
　　chicken thighs

2 (8-oz) cans of tomato
　　sauce or 16 oz of
　　fresh tomato sauce
　　(see Chapter 8)
1 cup cilantro, chopped
1/2 cup onion, chopped
1 garlic clove, minced

Heat 1 tablespoon of oil in skillet, add pepper rings, and fry until soft, about 15 minutes. Drain on absorbent towels. Add the remaining oil and the chicken and sauté until done, about 25–30 minutes.

Meanwhile, in a blender add the tomato sauce, cilantro, onion, and garlic. Blend well. Pour entire mixture over the chicken. When contents of pan boil, reduce heat, cover, and simmer for 5 minutes. When chicken is tender, serve with pepper rings on top.

6 servings

🐌

CHICKEN AND SQUASH WITH HERB BUTTER

It's the intermingled tarragon-butter flavors and the nicely crisped chicken skin that make this dish special. If you're just making 2 servings, use your toaster oven.

1/4 lb butter, soft
2 garlic cloves, minced
1/2 cup fresh basil,
   tarragon, or parsley,
   chopped

4 whole chicken legs
2 yellow squash, sliced
2 zucchini, sliced

Mix the butter, garlic, and herbs together. Refrigerate if desired.

Preheat the oven to 425° F. Dot the chicken under its skin with 4 tablespoons of the herb butter. Bake in the oven for 35 minutes.

Just before chicken is done, heat the rest of the herb butter in a large pan. Add squash and zucchini and sauté until tender, a few minutes at most. Serve the chicken surrounded by the squash.

4 servings

NOTE: Butter can be kept up to a month in the freezer.

❧

CHICKEN AND FRESH HERB PESTO

Another easy, delicious dinner. Guests love this one. I love this one. In fact, I'm hungry and I want some of it right now. Luckily, I just cooked this last night, so I have three legs left. I'm out of here.

4 green onions, cut into 1/2-inch pieces	2 Tbs walnut pieces or pine nuts
4 large garlic cloves	1-1/2 tsp grated lemon peel
1/2 cup fresh Italian parsley leaves	1/3 cup olive oil
1/4 cup fresh tarragon or basil leaves	4 whole chicken legs

Preheat the oven to 450° F.

Mix first 6 ingredients in a food processor. While machine is running, add oil slowly until mixture is a coarse paste.

Grease a baking dish. Put in chicken and spread with pesto. Bake until tender, about 40 minutes. Baste only once.

4 servings

⒔

BAKED CHICKEN WITH ROOT VEGETABLES

2 large carrots, peeled and
cut into 1-inch pieces
2 parsnips, peeled and cut
into 1-inch pieces
1 rutabaga, peeled and cut
into 1-inch pieces
1 medium onion, quartered

2 Tbs plus 2 tsps olive
oil
1 tsp sage
1 tsp dried rosemary
2 drumsticks and thigh
chicken pieces
2 garlic cloves, crushed

Preheat the oven to 375° F. Put the carrots, parsnips,
rutabaga, and onion in a baking pan. Add 2 tablespoons of oil,
1/2 teaspoon of sage, and 1/2 teaspoon rosemary. Stir all
ingredients. Bake covered for 30 minutes.

Meanwhile, rub the chicken with garlic, then with the
remaining oil, sage, and rosemary. Add the chicken to the
vegetables. Cook an additional hour, stirring the vegetables
occasionally.

2 servings

❧

CHICKEN À LA CHRIS

Your basic chicken sauté, and a tasty little sucker at that. If you want a treat sometime for your guests, try deglazing the pan with white wine instead of chicken broth.

4 chicken breast halves,
  skinned
1 Tbs olive oil
2 garlic cloves, minced
1 medium onion, chopped
1 red pepper, cut into
  strips

1 green pepper, cut into
  strips
1-1/2 cups chicken broth
1/4 cup tomato paste
1 Tbs cilantro, minced

Sauté the chicken in olive oil in a large pan until lightly browned on both sides. Remove the chicken. Add the garlic, onion, and peppers and cook for approximately 2 minutes. Add the chicken broth and tomato paste. Simmer covered 5 minutes. Return chicken to pan and simmer, uncovered, another 10 minutes. Stir in cilantro and serve.

4 servings

GRILLED TURKEY BROCHETTE

An old favorite around our house. The usual adjectives—quick, easy, delicious...

6 Tbs lemon juice
3 tsp sesame oil
8 oz turkey breast, cut into
   cubes

1 small zucchini, cut
   into chunks
1 red pepper, cored,
   seeded, and cut up
1 purple onion, peeled
   and cut into chunks

Combine lemon juice and oil in small bowl. Add turkey cubes and marinate in refrigerator for a minimum of 1 hour.

Thread turkey chunks onto skewers, alternating with vegetables. Grill 15 minutes, turning several times and basting with marinade.

2 servings

❧

ROAST CHICKEN WITH GARLIC

Nothing like a good, old-fashioned roast chicken. This one's particularly succulent.

1 3–4 lbs chicken	2 Tbs olive oil
10 large garlic cloves	3 Tbs chicken broth
1 Tbs dried oregano	

Preheat oven to 450° F.

Rinse chicken and pat dry. Place breast side up on foil-lined roasting pan. Split 8 garlic cloves and add, with 1/2 tablespoon of oregano, to chicken cavity.

Mince remaining garlic. Mix with remaining oregano, oil, and broth. Carefully separate skin from breast area of chicken, making pocket. Spoon half of garlic mixture into pocket and distribute evenly.

Smear remaining garlic mixture over surface of chicken. Tuck wings under chicken body and place in center of oven. Roast until juices from thigh have turned from rosy to clear, about 50 minutes. Let rest 10 minutes, then carve and serve.

4 servings

❧

TURKEY THIGHS WITH VEGETABLE SAUCE

1-1/2 cups chicken broth
3 lbs turkey thighs
1-1/2 Tbs oil or melted butter
1-1/2 tsp oregano
1/4 cup olive oil
1 onion, sliced
2 pattypan squash, sliced

2 yellow crookneck squash, sliced
1 bunch radish, cut in halves
2 Tbs fresh basil, chopped
Juice of 1 lemon
2 tomatoes, diced

Pour 1 cup of chicken broth into a shallow baking dish. Rub turkey thighs lightly with oil. Sprinkle with oregano and place in baking dish. Bake at 325° F for 60 minutes, basting occasionally.

Heat olive oil in a skillet and sauté onion until tender. Stir in pattypan squash, yellow squash, and radish. Sauté 3 minutes. Add remaining broth and lemon juice. Simmer until vegetables are tender-crisp. Add tomato and basil, stir until heated through.

Serve thighs with vegetables on side.

4 servings

Meat

Although we don't eat a lot of meat, we do have a few meat recipes that we couldn't live without.

❧

LAMB CHOPS WITH GARLIC AND ROSEMARY

As classic and elegant as a tuxedo. For your wine-freak friends, serve a flavorful California cabernet sauvignon.

2 or 4 3-inch-thick loin
    lamb chops, depending
    on appetite

2 branches fresh
    rosemary
2 garlic cloves, sliced
Olive oil to rub chops

Preheat broiler.

Rub chops with both garlic and rosemary. Poke slits with point of knife, 6 on each side of chop. Insert little bunches of rosemary needles in the slits on top, and thin slices of garlic in the ones on the bottom.

Tie chops around the perimeter with cotton string to prevent "tail" from drying. Rub with olive oil. Place 4 inches under heat in broiler. Broil 5 minutes per side, then begin checking for desired degree of doneness.

2 servings

🕰

LAMB CHOPS WITH TOMATO BUTTER

4 Tbs softened butter
1-1/2 whole sun-dried
   tomatoes

4 or 8 1-inch-thick
   shoulder lamb chops
2 Tbs minced parsley

Cream butter and tomatoes by hand or with a food processor. Put mixture in waxed paper and roll into a log. Chill at least an hour in the refrigerator.

Heat broiler. Broil chops 4 minutes per side until done. Sprinkle with parsley and top with a slice of butter.

4 servings

NOTE: Butter can be kept up to a month in the freezer.

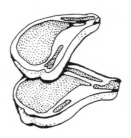

❧

GREEK LAMB

Even before there was CFS in our house, this was the one we cooked for guests when we were tired. No browning or anything—just toss the meat and other ingredients in your pan and bake. It comes out great every time.

You should get your butcher to do the cubing of the meat, as that is time consuming.

3 1/2 lbs lamb shoulder, cut into 1-inch cubes	1 tsp basil
2 garlic cloves	1/2 cup celery leaves, chopped
2/3 cup tomato paste (beware of sugar)	1/2 tsp dried oregano
1 large onion, chopped	1/2 cup dill, chopped
	1 cup parsley, chopped

Preheat the oven to 350° F. Put lamb into a large pan. Top with all other ingredients except half of basil and parsley. Toss to mix. Cover and cook for 1 hour.

Reduce oven to 300° F and cook for another 30 minutes, until the meat is tender. Sprinkle with the remaining herbs and serve.

4 servings

&❧

SKILLET LAMB WITH EGGPLANT

3 Tbs olive oil

2 lbs boneless lamb,
   shoulder or leg, cubed

2 large onions, sliced

1 eggplant, peeled and
   chopped

1/4 cup tomato puree

1 cup chicken broth

1 tomato, diced

Chopped parsley

Heat the oil in a large frying pan, add the meat and onions, and cook until onions are tender and meat is browned.

Add the eggplant to the lamb and brown lightly. Mix in the tomato puree and chicken broth. Cover and simmer for 45 minutes.

Serve, sprinkling each portion with tomato and parsley.

4 servings

ಜಿ

MEATBALLS WITH KALE

This recipe is delicious in an earthy, real-world sort of way—which is the way we like it. It is, however, somewhat labor-intensive, so this isn't one to take on if you're having a tired day. The work load can be made less onerous by making the meatballs earlier and keeping them in the fridge until ready to cook.

1/2 cup barley	3 Tbs finely chopped
1 Tbs unsalted butter	parsley
3/4 lb kale, stems removed,	1 egg, beaten
chopped	1/8 tsp nutmeg
1-1/4 cups chicken broth	2 tsp olive oil
1-1/2 lbs ground lamb	2 garlic cloves, crushed
1 medium onion, minced	1 tsp ground coriander

Cook the barley in a large pot of boiling water, partially covered, for 20 minutes. Drain and set aside.

At the same time, melt the butter in a large pot. Add the kale and 1/2 cup of chicken broth. Simmer for 20 minutes, covered.

Meanwhile, mix lamb, onion, parsley, egg, 1/4 cup chicken broth, and nutmeg in a large bowl. Stir well and shape into balls. If onion is not chopped finely enough, the balls will not hold together well.

Rub a heavy skillet with 1 teaspoon olive oil. Sauté the meatballs, a batch at a time, over medium-high heat until lightly browned on all sides.

Mash the garlic and coriander until a paste is formed. Heat the remaining teaspoon of oil in a small pan over medium heat. Add the garlic mixture and sauté for about 3 minutes.

Drain excess liquid from the kale, then stir in the garlic mixture. Add the barley, meatballs, and remaining half cup of chicken broth and mix well. Simmer, covered, for 30 minutes, adding more chicken broth or water if necessary.

6 servings

🍂

MEATBALL SHISH KEBABS

More grill-driven back-porch food. It's great—what's not to like?

1-1/2 lbs ground lamb
1 tsp dried mint
1/2 cup chopped parsley
2 garlic cloves, minced

16 chunks of red onion
16 cherry tomatoes
16 pieces of green bell
    pepper

Put the meat, mint, parsley, and garlic in a medium-sized bowl. Stir well. Shape the meat into 16 balls. Balls must be firm to prevent them from falling off skewers while cooking.

Place the meatballs onto skewers, alternating with onion chunks, tomatoes, and pepper pieces. Put the skewers into the refrigerator until ready to grill.

Cook over medium-hot coals or on cooktop grill, turning every 3 or 4 minutes until meat is done. This should take about 15 minutes in all.

6 servings

❧

MARINATED GRILLED RABBIT

Yes, Thumper. In addition to being cute, he happens to taste really good. Try it—it's like firmer chicken, with a lower fat content.

1 cup vegetable oil	1/2 tsp garlic salt
2 Tbs lemon juice	1 rabbit about 3 lbs, cut
1 tsp lemon peel, grated	in 6 pieces
1 tsp paprika	1 Tbs minced parsley
2 tsp fresh thyme	

Mix the oil, lemon juice, lemon peel, paprika, thyme, and garlic salt in a pan just big enough to hold all the rabbit pieces. Marinate the rabbit in the refrigerator for 1 hour, turning every 15 minutes.

Remove the rabbit from the marinade and grill slowly for 30 minutes. Use the remaining marinade for basting. When the rabbit is finished, serve on warm plates, pouring the remaining marinade over the rabbit.

6 servings

~ 8 ~

Sauces, Ingredients, and Accompaniments

Here are the adjusted versions of many of the sauces and other foods you took for granted before CFS. Also, some accompaniments to make eating more interesting, and even some dipping concoctions for corn chips to munch while you're watching TV.

❧

TOMATO SAUCE

Here's a good place to take advantage of the cans of already chopped, peeled tomatoes available these days in supermarkets. Why work if they're going to do it for you?

3 cups canned tomatoes,
chopped, most of the
juice discarded
1/2 tsp garlic powder

1/4 tsp rosemary,
minced
2 Tbs water

Combine tomatoes, garlic powder, rosemary, and water in a small saucepan. Bring to a boil.

Reduce heat and simmer, covered, stirring occasionally, until tomatoes are softened, about 4 minutes.

Serve warm or cold with almost anything.

3 cups

❧

MAYONNAISE

2 eggs   1-1/2 cups light olive oil
1 Tbs lemon juice

Put eggs and lemon juice in a blender or food processer and mix on high for 5 seconds. While machine is still running, slowly add oil in a steady stream. As it thickens, add the remaining oil quickly. Stop blender when mayonnaise is thick.

1-3/4 cups

❧

"VINAIGRETTE"

All right, it's not true vinaigrette. We're lying. But you can't have vinegar right now, so this'll have to do. Think of it as "lemonaigrette." It's pretty good. Use a good, flavorful olive oil, and you'll like this fine.

2 Tbs lemon juice   8 Tbs olive oil

In a small bowl mix lemon juice and olive oil. Taste it, and then add either more lemon juice or olive oil according to taste.

2/3 cup

NOTE: You may add minced garlic, shallots, onions, or any herb you might have handy to this basic recipe for an additional flavor element.

🙰

TAHINI SAUCE

Tahini is made entirely of sesame seeds. The sauce is wonderful as a dip, on rice cakes, or to spice up fish or chicken.

3/4 cup tahini (can be found in most health food stores and some supermarkets)

Juice of 3 or 4 lemons
1/2 tsp garlic powder

Add all ingredients and mix well. If sauce is too thick, add water until mixture reaches proper consistency.

1 cup

🎜

PEPPER-AVOCADO SALSA

This is a great dip with corn chips, or to serve with chicken, fish, or even meat. If you're feeling tired, don't bother roasting and peeling the peppers—it's an annoying task. Have someone else do it, or use them just seeded.

2 Tbs olive oil
1/2 cup chopped onions
2 garlic cloves, chopped
1 lb tomatillos, peeled and
    quartered
1 lb plum tomatoes,
    quartered
1/2 tsp ground cumin

1 red bell pepper,
    roasted, peeled, and
    seeded
1 green bell pepper,
    roasted, peeled, and
    seeded
1/2 avocado, chopped
1 Tbs cilantro, chopped

Put olive oil in large pan over medium heat. Add onions, garlic, tomatillos, tomatoes, and cumin and cook for 20 minutes. Add peppers and place the entire mixture in a food processor or blender and blend coarsely with on-off pulses. Pour in bowl and bring to room temperature; mix in the avocado and cilantro.

2 quarts

❧

SIMPLE SALSA

For a different flavor element, try adding chopped tomatoes. This salsa will last about a week in the refrigerator.

1 ripe avocado, chopped
   into 1/4-inch pieces
3 Tbs olive oil
2-1/2 Tbs lime juice

1/3 cup green onions,
   chopped
1 garlic clove, crushed
2 Tbs fresh cilantro,
   chopped

In a medium bowl, combine all ingredients. Stir well.

2 cups

❧

HOLLANDAISE

It's nice that a luxurious item like this is 100 percent okay for your diet. Have it on vegetables, eggs Benedict, and so forth.

1/4 cup butter   2 tsp lemon juice
2 egg yolks

Melt butter in saucepan. In a blender, blend egg yolks and lemon juice. Use low speed. Remove the cover and continue to blend, while adding the butter in a steady, narrow stream. Hollandaise will thicken. When all the butter has been added, sauce is ready to serve.

3/4 cup

 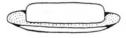

ខ

MARINARA SAUCE

This is the best marinara sauce I've ever tasted. Lush, sweet, fabulous. Who says you're deprived?

1-1/2 cups onion, chopped
1 carrot, diced
3 Tbs olive oil
4 garlic cloves, crushed

1 28-oz can tomato
    puree
3 Tbs fresh basil,
    chopped
1 tsp dried oregano

Sauté the onions and carrot in olive oil until onions are tender. When almost finished, add the garlic. Then add the tomato puree, basil, and oregano. Cook over low-medium heat until thickened, about 20 minutes.

3 cups

🍃

MICROWAVE CHICKEN STOCK

The oven cooking bags may burst open during the microwave cooking. Read package directions carefully.

1 chicken, about 3 lbs	1 bay leaf
1 onion, quartered	1 thyme sprig
2 celery stalks, quartered	Oven cooking bags
1 medium carrot, quartered	3 cups water

Stuff chicken with as much of other ingredients as you can fit in. Put in oven cooking bag, and put bag in large, microwave-safe bowl. Add 3 cups water to the bag and tie a loose knot to close it.

Microwave on high 20 minutes, more if chicken weighs more than 3 pounds. Turn over halfway through cooking. Reduce power to defrost and cook another 15 minutes. Strain stock, remove and discard vegetables. Save poached chicken for chicken salad.

(Times should be increased by 50 percent for smaller ovens.)

3 cups

PART THREE

The Phase Two Diet

The Phase Two Diet

Congratulations! You've worked hard to eat the right foods. You should be feeling much better than you did four months ago. Now your reward: a more diverse diet. Try these recipes and experiment with some of your own.

Remember to reintroduce new foods one at a time and gauge your response to them. If you continue to have a problem, discontinue that particular food.

∾ 9 ∾

Breakfast

Even now you must be endlessly careful about cereal. Maybe only one in fifty is made without sugar. Puffed wheat, corn, and millet cereals can be found that contain nothing but wheat, corn, or millet. It's worth the search—they taste good with goat's milk and fruit. For suggestions on some allowable cereals see our list in Chapter 3.

In fact, if you find that you can now tolerate fruit, it makes a nice breakfast all by itself. Honeydew melon with lime is a major treat. Mango for breakfast is close to sin. The one caveat—you'll probably run out of fuel halfway through the morning, so have some nuts or other snacks on hand when the munchies strike.

Also remember that fresh-juiced fruit is delicious. Juiced honeydew with lime, for instance, is awesome. Experiment with your own mixtures. Remember, though, it must be *fresh*, either juiced yourself or at a health food store or juice bar. V-8 and the like won't do.

🍎

"STANDARD" BREAKFAST

This is an ultra-easy breakfast that never gets tiresome. I have it almost every day.

1/2 cup corn cereal (can be bought at health food stores and some supermarkets)

1/4 cup goat's milk
1/2 banana

Pour cereal into a bowl, top with goat's milk, and add banana.

1 serving

🍎

BREAKFAST COUSCOUS

2 cups water
1/4 tsp cinnamon

1 cup instant couscous
Butter

In a medium saucepan, combine the water and cinnamon and bring to a boil. Pour in the couscous, reduce the heat to a simmer, and cook for 30 seconds.

Remove from heat, cover, and let stand for at least 5 minutes, until the liquid is absorbed. Top with butter and serve.

2 servings

&.

CRANBERRY TUMBLER

1/2 cup unsweetened
 cranberry juice
1/2 cup seltzer water

1/2 tsp lemon juice
Sprig of mint

Mix together in glass.

1 serving

&.

YOGURT AND FRUIT

Another of our difficult, complex recipes. Think of this as the under-5-minute breakfast. Just be aware that halfway through the morning you'll probably find yourself starving, so be prepared with a snack that'll get you through to lunch.

2 cups goat's milk yogurt
1/2 cup papaya, diced

1/2 cup pineapple, diced
1/2 cup bananas, diced
1/4 tsp cinnamon

Put the yogurt in a large mixing bowl. Add the fruit and sprinkle with cinnamon.

4 servings

NOTE: Use just one fruit or as many as you like.

❧

CURRIED EGGS

This curry sauce is soooooo good. How good, you ask? Our friend Leslie leaves out the eggs, makes just the sauce, and keeps it in her refrigerator to pour on rice, vegetables, or Peter, her husband. May we make a suggestion? This you want to eat.

3 Tbs butter	1/4 tsp cayenne pepper
6 hard-boiled eggs, peeled and sliced lengthwise	1/4 tsp ground cloves
	1/4 tsp ground ginger
1/2 tsp mustard seeds	1/2 cup goat's milk
1/2 tsp ground cumin	yogurt
1/2 tsp ground turmeric	1/4 cup sesame seeds

Preheat broiler.

Brush a pie pan with 1 tablespoon of melted butter. Place the egg slices face up in the pie pan.

Melt the two remaining tablespoons of butter in a small pan. Add the mustard seeds and cook for 2 minutes or until they pop. Add the cumin, turmeric, cayenne, cloves, and ginger.

Whisk the yogurt until smooth. Add the spiced butter, mix well, and spoon on top of the eggs. Sprinkle with sesame seeds and broil until bubbly, about 5 minutes.

4 servings

&.

CHEESE AND CHIVE POLENTA

Other ingredients may be added—corn kernels, chopped onion, red bell pepper in small dice, etc. Your imagination's the limit.

3 cups chicken broth
1-1/4 cups cornmeal
1/4 cup chives, minced
2 Tbs parsley, minced

4 Tbs butter
1/2 cup goat cheese,
   crumbled

Bring the broth to boil in a large frying pan. Gradually whisk in the cornmeal. Lower heat and cook, stirring constantly until mixture starts to thicken.

Immediately whisk in the chives, parsley, cheese, and 2 tablespoons of butter. When the cornmeal has thickened, dot with remaining 2 tablespoons of butter.

You can serve the polenta as is or, for a special treat, broil it for a few minutes until golden brown. Or allow to harden, cut, and sauté in olive oil.

4 servings

NOTE: Leave out the goat cheese and this recipe is a perfect Phase One hit.

CORNMEAL PANCAKES

1-1/2 cups cornmeal
1/4 cup rice flour
1 tsp baking soda
2 cups goat's milk

2 Tbs butter, melted
1 egg, separated
1 tsp vegetable oil

In a medium bowl, combine the cornmeal, flour, and baking soda. Add the goat's milk, butter, and egg yolk. Stir until all the ingredients are moistened. (The batter should not be perfectly smooth.)

Beat the egg white until stiff but not dry. Fold into the batter.

Heat the oil on a griddle or large skillet. Spoon the batter onto the hot griddle to form 4 pancakes. Cook until bubbles form on the surface of the pancakes, about 2 minutes. Flip and cook 2 more minutes on the other side.

Serve with butter and top with yummy fruits.

4 servings

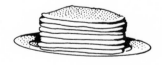

❧

CORNMEAL PIE

This is a great recipe to make and just have in the refrigerator, ready for snacking or a throw-together meal. "Mexican Seasoning" is a mixture of herbs and spices you can probably find at your supermarket—it adds flavor interest to this dish.

3 cups water
1 cup cornmeal
1 cup goat's milk
1 Tbs olive oil
1/2 cup celery, diced
1 onion, chopped
1/2 green pepper, chopped
1 cup tomatoes, chopped

1/2 cup corn kernels, fresh or frozen
1 Tbs "Mexican Seasoning"
1-1/2 cups leftover meat or poultry, minced
1 cup goat's cheese, grated

Preheat oven to 325° F. Meanwhile, over high heat boil water in a large saucepan. Mix cornmeal with goat's milk; add to boiling water. Stir and cook over medium heat until thickened. Then cover and simmer for 10 minutes. Pour into a baking dish.

Heat oil in a skillet, add celery, onion, and green pepper, and cook for 10 minutes. Add remaining ingredients except for the cheese and simmer for 5 more minutes. Pour vegetable mixture over the cornmeal and sprinkle the cheese on top. Bake for 45 minutes.

4 servings

∿ 10 ∿

Lunch

∂🐌

CHILLED TOMATO SOUP

*Amazing that anything this easy to throw together can taste so good.
You'll smack your lips and roll your eyes.*

1 cup goat's milk yogurt	1 cucumber, sliced and
1 Tbs lemon juice	the slices quartered
3 cups fresh tomato juice	(if desired)

Whisk yogurt until it's thin and smooth. Add the lemon juice
and whisk again. Add the tomato juice and stir well. Stir in
the cucumber. Chill in refrigerator.

4 servings

❧

TABBOULEH

This dish is fresher than springtime. All I can say is that it just feels good going down. In fact, Chris says it's better than any tabbouleh he's had from any store anywhere in the world.

1 cup boiling water	1 large tomato, chopped
1/2 cup bulgur wheat	6 sprigs mint, chopped
1-1/2 cups fresh parsley, chopped	Juice of 1-1/2 lemons
4 green onions, chopped	1/4 cup olive oil

Pour boiling water over bulgur wheat. Let stand for 1 hour. In a large bowl, mix parsley, green onions, tomato, mint, and bulgur wheat. Then add lemon juice and olive oil and mix well.

4 servings

ﻰ

CUCUMBER CURRY SALAD

You can leave out the draining-of-the-cucumber step if you wish.
You probably won't notice the difference.

This is a wonderfully crunchy, tangy, Middle-Eastern-tasting
thing that's a big hit with guests. It's great.

1-1/2 tsp ground cumin
1/2 tsp celery seeds
1/2 tsp mustard seeds
1/2 tsp ground coriander
1/2 tsp ground cardamom
2 cups plain goat's milk
   yogurt

3 cucumbers, halved, cut
   lengthwise into
   strips, and then cut
   into 1-inch pieces
1 tsp salt
1/2 cup fresh parsley,
   chopped
1/2 cup scallions, sliced

In a small skillet, combine spices and toast over medium heat,
stirring constantly for 3 minutes. Pour in bowl. When cool,
add yogurt and stir well. Cover and refrigerate.

Toss cucumbers with salt and set aside for 1 hour to drain.
Then pat dry.

When ready to serve, toss cucumbers with parsley, 1/4
cup of scallions, and the yogurt mixture. Sprinkle with
remaining scallions.

10 servings

🐌

SPECIAL QUESADILLAS

2/3 cup corn kernels
1 tsp water
2 large green onions, thinly
     sliced

2 Tbs cilantro leaves
2 tsp vegetable oil
4 flour tortillas
8 oz goat cheese
Simple Salsa (see
     Chapter 8)

Combine corn, water, green onions, and cliantro leaves in a
small bowl. Heat half the oil in a large skillet. Place one
tortilla in the skillet. Cover with a layer of cheese, top with
some of the corn mixture, and layer on more cheese. Top with
another tortilla and cook approximately 3 minutes on each
side.

Repeat for second quesadilla. Cut tortillas into wedges.
Serve with salsa.

2 servings

🐌

SPECIAL BURGERS

A sort of Mideastern thing, with bold flavors and a nice crunchy texture. With catsup, it's an easy sell to your kids.

3/4 cup boiling water
1/4 cup bulgur wheat
1/3 cup whole natural almonds
1 lb mixed lean ground turkey

1/4 cup vegetable oil
1/4 cup red onion, chopped
1 tsp garlic salt
1 tsp dried basil leaves

Preheat oven to 350° F. Pour water over the bulgur and let stand until cool.

Put the almonds in a single layer on a baking sheet. Bake for 15 minutes, stirring occasionally, until lightly toasted. Cool, then chop.

Drain bulgur well. Then add the almonds, meat, oil, red onion, garlic, and basil and mix well. Shape into 6 patties. Grill, broil, or sauté until meat is done to your taste.

6 servings

&⅞

GREEK BURGERS

1/4 cup vegetable oil
1-1/2 lbs mixed ground
    turkey
1/4 cup green onions,
    chopped

1 tsp dried oregano
    leaves, crumbled
1/2 tsp garlic powder
2 oz feta cheese,
    crumbled
Juice of 1 lemon

Add oil to ground turkey, mix well. Add the remaining ingredients and mix well. Shape into 6 patties.

Fry or grill patties, about 6 minutes per side, until meat reaches desired doneness.

6 servings

🍽

MEATBALL, SPINACH, AND BEAN STEW

An extremely "satisfying" dinner was the consensus on this one when we served it to guests. Let's see, it tasted really good...it was "real food" that stuck to the ribs...it was unusual, vaguely ethnic, mysterious...

1/3 cup split peas	1/2 butternut squash,
1/3 cup black-eyed peas	peeled and chopped
1/3 cup lentils	1 bunch spinach,
1 lb ground lamb	chopped
2 garlic cloves, minced	2 cups goat's milk
1 onion, minced	yogurt
2 Tbs olive oil	4 Tbs dried mint flakes

Rinse peas and lentils until water runs clear. Soak for 2 hours in water just to cover.

Mix the lamb, garlic, and onion, and form into little meatballs. Brown over medium heat in olive oil.

Simmer the peas, lentils, and squash over low heat in the same water for 45 minutes or until peas are tender. Don't boil; add water, as necessary. When done, discard most of the water. Add the meatballs and spinach, mixing well, and let simmer 15 additional minutes. Turn off the heat, stir in the yogurt and mint flakes. Serve.

4 servings

❧

EGGPLANT WITH MARINARA SAUCE

This is as delicious a recipe as you'll find in this whole book. Sweet, luscious, flavorful. Really a knockout. Eggplant and olive oil are one of God's great flavor combinations. If you're in a hurry, or feeling tired, just grill or broil the slices painted with olive oil. Forget the sauce—they're delicious just like that.

1 large eggplant, sliced thinly

1/2 cup olive oil, more as needed

1 cup Marinara Sauce (see Chapter 8)

2 large tomatoes, thinly sliced

8 oz goat cheese, thinly sliced

Fresh or dried basil leaves to taste

Fresh or dried oregano leaves to taste

Preheat oven to 350° F.

Prepare eggplant slices by painting them with a good olive oil and either broiling or grilling them. You may also sauté them in olive oil. Slices are done when they are browned.

Pour half of the Marinara Sauce in a shallow baking dish. Put eggplant slices in the dish and place a tomato slice and a cheese slice on top of each eggplant slice. Cover with remaining Marinara Sauce and season with basil and oregano leaves. Heat in the oven for 5–10 minutes—until heated through.

8 servings

🌶

STUFFED YELLOW PEPPERS

6 oz soft goat cheese, cut
    into 5 equal pieces
4 large sweet yellow pep-
    pers, cored and seeded.
    Save tops

1 bunch basil leaves
2 large plum tomatoes,
    sliced
2 Tbs olive oil

Press 1 piece of goat cheese into the bottom of each yellow
pepper. Top with 2 basil leaves. Add tomato slices on top of
basil, then layer 2 more basil leaves and drizzle some olive oil
in each pepper. Crumble last piece of goat cheese on top of the
peppers and replace the tops.

Rub the outside of the peppers with remaining olive oil
and wrap in foil. Grill over medium heat for 20-30 minutes,
turning every 5 minutes, or if using an indoor grill, grill on
high for 30-45 minutes until cheese is soft.

4 servings

ᥱ 11 ᥲ

Dinner

ᥱᥲ
COUSCOUS WITH SAGE

A nicely different way to put a grain on the plate.

1/2 cup chicken broth
1/2 tsp crumbled dried
sage

1/2 cup couscous
2 tsp unsalted butter,
chopped

In a small saucepan boil chicken broth and sage, then stir in couscous and remove from heat. Let the couscous stand, covered, for 5 minutes, then add the butter. Fluff with a fork and serve.

2 servings

🐦

PILAF WITH CASHEWS

1 medium onion, thinly
    sliced
1 Tbs butter
1/2 cup bulgur

3/4 cup chicken broth
3 Tbs chopped dry-
    roasted, unsalted
    cashews
1 Tbs scallions, chopped

In a small saucepan, cook onion in butter until tender. Add bulgur and cook, stirring constantly, for about 1 minute. Add the broth, bring to a boil, and then simmer, covered, for 10 minutes or until liquid is absorbed.

Transfer pilaf to a bowl. Sprinkle with cashews and scallions.

2 servings

&.

AVOCADO PASTA

At first the idea of avocado with pasta didn't sound quite right to me. It seemed a bizarre combination. But it turned out to be so good that when we served it to our friend Leslie, it actually turned her mood around, despite the fact that she'd just been given a $250 ticket for leaving her car momentarily in a handicapped parking space. Now, that's good.

8 oz pasta
1/4 cup olive oil
1-1/2 lbs tomatoes, seeded
    and diced
3 oz goat cheese, crumbled

1 large avocado, diced
1/2 cup onion, diced
4 garlic cloves, minced
1 Tbs fresh parsley,
    chopped
1 Tbs fresh basil,
    chopped

Cook the pasta in boiling water until *al dente*, following package directions. Drain.

Mix together the olive oil, tomatoes, cheese, avocado, onion, garlic, parsley, and basil in a large bowl.

Add the pasta and mix well.

4 servings

❧

RAVIOLI WITH TOMATO AND GARLIC SAUCE

A lot of these recipes can be made even shorter and simpler. In this one, for instance, you can buy olives that're already pitted. And you don't have to worry about peeling and seeding the tomatoes—they'll be fine just chopped. The ravioli you can buy already made; all you have to do is cook it. You can even buy garlic that's already been minced. Feeling tired? Be good to yourself and do it the easy way.

1/4 cup olive oil
6 garlic cloves, minced
12 plum tomatoes, peeled, seeded, and chopped
2 lbs fresh chicken ravioli

1/2 cup black Mediterranean olives, pitted and halved
2/3 cup parsley, chopped
Grated goat cheese

Heat the oil in a saucepan over medium heat. Add the garlic and cook until soft, about 3 minutes. Add the tomatoes, raise the heat to high, and cook about 10 more minutes.

Cook the ravioli. Drain. Meanwhile, reheat the garlic and tomato mixture if cold. Remove from heat; add the olives and parsley.

Top the ravioli with the garlic and tomato mixture. Serve with grated goat cheese.

4 servings

❧

PASTA WITH TOMATO BASIL SAUCE

Simple. Easy. Delicious. Recipes like this are what this book is about.

1 lb pasta
1/2 cup olive oil
6 garlic cloves, pureed
6 large tomatoes, diced
2 Tbs basil, chopped

1/2 cup goat's cheese,
    crumbled
1 tsp parsley, chopped
3/4 cup toasted pine
    nuts (optional)

Cook the pasta in boiling water, until *al dente*, according to package directions. Drain. Add 1 tablespoons of olive oil and stir.

Meanwhile, sauté half the garlic in a large skillet using 2 tablespoons of olive oil. Cook over medium heat for 1 minute. Add the tomatoes and basil. Bring to a boil, then reduce heat and simmer for 40 minutes or until the sauce begins to thicken.

In a separate pan, sauté the remaining garlic in the remaining olive oil. Cook for 1 minute. Add the pasta and toss over high heat until heated through. Sprinkle with cheese and most of the parsley and mix well. Transfer to a hot serving platter. Top with tomato sauce. Garnish with pine nuts (optional) and remaining parsley.

6 servings

🐌

ORZO WITH ONION

Orzo—the pasta that looks like rice! It's slick stuff, and this is a nice little recipe.

1 garlic clove, minced	1-1/2 Tbs olive oil
2 cups water	1 onion, chopped
1 cup orzo	1 Tbs parsley, minced

Bring the garlic and water to a boil in a heavy saucepan. Add the orzo and return to boil. Reduce heat and simmer until orzo is tender, about 10 minutes. Remove from heat and drain. Then add the oil, onion, and parsley and mix well.

4 servings

❧

GREEK RAINBOW TROUT

2 rainbow trout fillets
1 small tomato, chopped
1/2 cup goat cheese,
    crumbled
2 Tbs Greek olives, sliced

2 tsp fresh basil,
    chopped, or 1 tsp
    dried
2 tsp olive oil
1/4 cup lemon juice
Lemon slices

Put the trout in a microwave dish. Sprinkle with tomato, cheese, olives, and basil. Drizzle with olive oil and lemon juice.

Microwave on high, covered, for 2 minutes. Rotate the dish and cook 5–10 minues longer on high until fish is done. Garnish with lemon slices.

2 servings

❧

SWORDFISH WITH GRAPEFRUIT AND ROSEMARY BUTTER SAUCE

Okay, this is a strikingly great-tasting dish. If you have company coming you want to impress, make this and serve it with an upscale chardonnay, not too oaky. Or a white burgundy with a bit of acid, or a chablis. This dish, with those wines, will evoke whimpers of pleasure from anyone alive. And of course, you may enjoy a glass of sparkling, crisp seltzer water.

3 Tbs butter
2 4-oz swordfish steaks
2 shallots, minced

1 tsp dried rosemary, crumbled
3/4 cup fresh grapefruit juice
Fresh parsley sprigs

Melt 1 tablespoon butter in a heavy skillet over medium heat. Add the fish and cook until it reaches desired doneness. Transfer to a warm platter and cover to keep warm.

Add the shallots and rosemary, stirring over medium heat until the shallots soften, about 2 minutes. Add the grapefruit juice and bring to a boil, scraping up all bits. Boil until sauce is the consistency of syrup, about 3 to 4 minutes.

Remove from the heat and add 2 tablespoons butter, 1 tablespoon at a time, stirring until butter is melted. Spoon the sauce over the fish and garnish with parsley.

2 servings

❧

SCALLOPS WITH ORANGE-GINGER SAUCE

There are three kinds of sesame oil. The first is hot *sesame oil, which will turn your neck into the hot side of the planet Mercury. The second is plain, golden-colored sesame oil—it has no particular character and could be any oil. What you want is* toasted *sesame oil, which you can find at your local health food store. This is wonderfully flavorful stuff, and really makes the recipe work.*

3 Tbs *fresh* orange juice (most concentrates add sugar)	1-1/2 tsp cornstarch
	1-1/2 tsp sesame oil
	3/4 lb bay scallops
1-1/2 Tbs lemon juice	2 Tbs butter
1-1/2 tsp gingerroot, grated	

In a small bowl mix orange juice, lemon juice, ginger root, cornstarch, and sesame oil. Dip scallops in cornstarch mixture, coat well, and sauté in butter for 3 minutes.

Remove scallops to warmed serving plate. Add orange juice mixture to pan, raise heat to high, and reduce until thick. Pour over scallops and serve.

2 servings

🐚

BROILED FISH WITH CAPER SAUCE

4 boneless fish fillets (about 1-1/2 lbs)	2 tsp balsamic vinegar
	1-1/2 tsp capers, rinsed
4 Tbs butter	1 Tbs parsley, minced

Preheat the broiler. Broil the fish about 6 inches from the heat for 3–5 minutes.

In a small saucepan, melt the butter over moderately low heat. Add the vinegar and capers and cook until heated through, about 1 minute. Remove from heat and stir in the parsley. Spoon over fillets and serve.

4 servings

🐦

LEMON CHICKEN WITH CAPERS

This dish defines "elegant." A truly delicious, easy, and healthy recipe—I could eat something like this every night. For those of you unafflicted with CFS, you'll find this goes like gangbusters with a young California chardonnay.

1/4 cup pine nuts
4 chicken breast halves,
   boned, skin on or off
1 Tbs extra-virgin olive oil
1/2 cup chicken broth

1-1/2 Tbs fresh lemon
   juice
1 Tbs capers
3 Tbs butter

Toast pine nuts in 400° F oven or toaster oven. It won't take long, maybe 2–3 minutes, so keep an eye on them. Set aside to cool.

Gently pound the breasts between sheets of waxed paper until flattened. In a large skillet, heat the oil over moderately high heat until almost smoking. Add breasts, skin-side down, and cook until golden brown, about 5 minutes. Turn over and cook until white thoughout but still moist, an additional 3 minutes. Arrange the chicken on a large platter. Cover with foil to keep warm. Pour off fat from skillet.

Add chicken broth and bring to a boil, scraping up any brown bits from the bottom of the pan. Cook over high heat until reduced by half, about 3 minutes. Add the lemon juice and capers. Remove from heat and whisk in butter, 1 tablespoon at a time. Pour any accumulated juices from the chicken platter into the sauce. Pour sauce over the chicken and sprinkle with pine nuts.

4 servings

CHICKEN PROVENCAL

It's page 201! How many more ways are there to say something is quick, easy, and delicious? I'm going to start saying "Q.E.D.," okay? And you'll know what I mean—"quick, easy, delicious." You got that? I just can't type "quick, easy, delicious" again.

2 chicken breast halves,
  skinned and boned
1 Tbs olive oil
4 Tbs butter
4 oz goat cheese

2 small tomatoes, sliced
1 Tbs chopped fresh
  rosemary or 3/4 tsp
  dried
1/2 cup chicken broth

Place the breast halves between sheets of waxed paper. Pound with a meat hammer until flattened.

Over medium-high heat, heat oil and 2 tablespoons butter in a large skillet. Sauté breasts until golden on both sides. Arrange alternating slices of cheese and tomato on each breast. Sprinkle with rosemary. Pour broth over chicken and cover.

Lower heat and cook for about 3 minutes, until cheese and tomato are cooked through. Cheese should not melt completely. Remove chicken to warm platter. Over high heat, boil sauce rapidly down. Stir in 2 remaining tablespoons of butter, one at a time. Pour sauce over chicken.

4 servings

❧

CHICKEN CURRY

8 chicken thighs, skinned
1 cup goat's milk yogurt
1 tsp ground ginger
1/2 tsp ground turmeric
1 tsp garlic, minced
1 cup vegetable oil
2 onions, chopped
1 Tbs ground coriander
1 Tbs ground cumin
1 Tbs ground almonds
1/2 cup shredded coconut
1/4 tsp ground nutmeg

1/4 tsp ground mace
1/2 tsp ground
 cinnamon
1/2 tsp ground cloves
1 Tbs ground cardamom
1 cup warm water
2 Tbs goat's milk
1/4 tsp saffron
1/2 cup cilantro leaves,
 chopped
1/4 cup lemon juice

Pierce the chicken thighs with a fork. Then mix together the yogurt, ginger, turmeric, and garlic. Rub over the chicken and marinate in the refrigerator for 2 hours.

Heat the oil in a large skillet and sauté the onions until golden. Reserving the oil, remove the onions and set aside to cool. In the same skillet cook the coriander, cumin, almonds, coconut, nutmeg, and mace over medium-low heat for 3 minutes, stirring constantly. Put the onion and coriander mix in a blender and grind to a fine paste. Transfer to a large bowl and add the cinnamon, cloves, and cardamom. Stir.

Reheat the oil from the onions and cook the chicken until done, about 20–25 minutes. Pour the spice paste over the chicken and top with any leftover yogurt marinade. Add the warm water and simmer until the chicken is tender. In a small saucepan, warm the milk and add the saffron. When heated through, add it gradually to the chicken, stirring slowly, cooking 2 more minutes. Before serving sprinkle the chicken with cilantro and lemon juice.

Serve with rice.

4 servings

❧

TURKEY MEAT LOAF

Our friend Paula taste-tested this recipe and had two things to say about it: Great and easy. Or Q.E.D., as we are now saying.

2 lbs ground turkey
1-1/2 cups fresh whole-
 wheat bread crumbs
1/2 cup red onion, finely
 chopped
1/2 cup red pepper, finely
 chopped

1 can (6-oz) tomato
 paste
2 eggs, beaten
1/4 cup parsley, chopped
2 tsp sage
4 garlic cloves, minced
1 Tbs lemon juice

Preheat oven to 350° F. Combine all ingredients into a large bowl. Mix well. Shape into 2 loaves and place in baking pans. Bake at 350° F for about 1 hour.

6 servings

TURKEY WITH GREEN PEPPERCORN SAUCE

One of the Q.E.D.-est dinners in this book. Turkey breast slices by themselves don't have a lot of flavor. It's all in the sauce you use. This broth-onion-mustard-peppercorn one is delicious, but you can probably think of other mixtures. Olives-broth-garlic, for instance. Or one of the sauce recipes in this book—tomato, marinara...

1-1/4 lbs turkey breast
   slices
1 Tbs vegetable oil
2 Tbs butter
1 cup chicken broth

3 green onions, minced
1 Tbs Dijon mustard
1/2 Tbs green pepper-
   corns

Put turkey slices between sheets of wax paper and pound with meat tenderizing mallet.

Heat oil and butter in a large skillet and sauté turkey slices 2 minutes on each side. Remove and keep warm.

Simmer chicken broth, green onions, mustard, and peppercorns in same skillet for 5 minutes. Keep heat low, or sauce will boil away. Return turkey slices to pan until warmed through, toss with sauce, and serve.

6 servings

❧

TURKEY SCALLOPS WITH CHEESE
AND ARTICHOKE PUREE

1-1/2 Tbs butter
1-1/2 Tbs olive oil
8 turkey scallops (about
    1 lb)

1 jar (6 oz) marinated
    artichoke hearts,
    drained and pureed
4 oz goat's cheese,
    grated

Heat broiler. Heat butter and olive oil in a large skillet. Add scallops; sauté until browned on both sides, about 3–5 minutes. Transfer scallops to a large baking pan. Spread a thin layer of artichoke puree on each scallop. Top with pieces of cheese.

Broil until cheese is golden and bubbly, about 4 minutes.

4 servings

❧

CURRIED LAMB WITH ORANGES

If you're feeling fancy, you could garnish this with orange slices. If you're tired, forget it.

This is a great-tasting entrée, a real crowd-pleaser. For you wine buffs, go with a cabernet sauvignon or bordeaux. The orange flavors seem to punch up the wine's flavors.

1 lb lamb, trimmed of fat and cut in 1-inch squares	1 onion, chopped
	2 garlic cloves, minced
	Juice of 1 orange
2 tsp vegetable oil	1 Tbs curry powder

Sauté lamb in one teaspoon of the oil until browned on all sides. Set aside and keep warm.

Sauté the onion and garlic in remaining oil until the onion is tender. Add the orange juice and curry powder and stir until smooth. Cover and simmer for 8 minutes over low heat. If too dry, add more juice or a little water.

Arrange lamb on plates and cover with sauce.

6 servings

🐚

VEAL CHOPS WITH HERBED ORANGE BUTTER

A nice, elegant entrée. Try it with a pinot noir or red burgundy (you wine-drinkers) that has some acidity. It plays off the lemon juice in the butter, making a nice match.

1/4 cup unsalted butter, softened
1/2 tsp orange rind, grated
1 tsp lemon rind, grated
1 tsp lemon juice
2 tsp shallot, minced

1/4 tsp garlic, minced
2 Tbs fresh basil leaves, chopped
2 Tbs olive oil
4 1-inch-thick rib veal chops (10 oz each)

Leave butter out to soften.

Mix the first 7 ingredients in a small mixing bowl. Chill 15 minutes. Roll into log, wrap in wax paper, and refrigerate another hour. (Make butter in advance if you wish.)

In a large pan heat the oil over high heat until it is hot but not smoking. Sauté the veal chops, about 10 minutes or until meat is done to your taste, turning once.

Cut butter into half-inch slices and place on chops.

4 servings

NOTE: Butter can be made and kept up to a month in the freezer.

∽ Appendix ∾

Food You Don't Cook Yourself

As we noted earlier, the world was not set up for people who need this diet. Trying to order at restaurants can be infuriating—there's not *one thing* you can eat. Delis and fast food outlets drive you crazy. The general outlook in ready-to-eat food is grim.

But it's not a total loss. What there *is* available to you, we'll try to summarize here.

Restaurants

You should *always* ask at restaurants about the ingredients in things. Does the tomato sauce contain sugar? Is there vinegar anywhere in what you're ordering? Don't be afraid to be a pain in the neck. Make the waiter go to the kitchen and ask if he doesn't know. Eventually, you'll get a dinner you can eat.

Mexican is a good bet. You'll need to specify corn tortillas instead of flour, but the rice and beans are right on the mark. You have to be careful about cheese; request it be left off.

Chinese is deadly. Almost everything has soy sauce or sugar on it. Likewise, Thai food. You can get by fairly well in a Japanese restaurant; just ask questions and read the menu carefully. Sushi, unfortunately, is a problem—the green mustard is a no-no, and raw fish may contain parasites. Parasites are all too common in people with immune-suppressed disorders, and this is one additional problem you don't need.

Middle Eastern restaurants serve falafel, which is made from vegetables. Served with tahini sauce, it's delicious.

Usually they give you a salad; ask for oil and lemon juice instead of whatever other dressing they use. Hummus (chick peas) is also on the approved list.

Grill restaurants are good. Grilled fish, chops, and the like are simple, delicious, and dietetically correct. Likewise, seafood restaurants. Just be sure to ask what seasonings and other ingredients may be used.

At other restaurants, it's catch-as-catch-can. In some cases, you can work with the kitchen to custom-make something for you. Sometimes this is not an option. Patience and fortitude are called for.

Take-out

As with restaurant eating, you'll probably do best with Mexican, Middle Eastern, and seafood take-out. If you're on the Phase Two diet you can even try various fried chicken places—however, fried chicken is often dipped in a wheat batter before cooking, and wheat is not allowed if you're allergic to it. Fried foods are on the forbidden list, but in an emergency (when you're too tired to deal with anything else), you can get by with them.

Remember—always ask about ingredients. Don't assume any food is okay until you know it is.

Delicatessen

These are the ready-to-eat foods you can buy at a deli or in the deli section of a supermarket. As with all other sources, you'll have to check ingredients, and it's going to be difficult finding much you can eat.

One of our local health food markets carries something called "Brown Rice Salad." It's brown rice, vegetables, and olive oil, and is fine. They also have tabbouleh.

A Final Note

It has been our pleasure to put this book together for you. Eight years of our lives have been devoted to grappling with an immune system disease and how to eat to help combat it.

Believe us when we tell you that we know the hardships, discomforts, and pain you must go through to get back to what you once believed was your birthright: an active, healthy life. The long, winding steps *are* difficult and uncertain. The medical community does not believe you, the insurance company doesn't want to pay your bills, and all too often you don't even have the energy to get out of bed and face the day. But you can do it, and we only hope this book will help you reachieve and keep the blessed gift of health. Your journey *will* be difficult, but it will be rewarded.

With much love,

Mary and Chris

Index